IMAGES OF WAR

THE NAZIS' WINTER WARFARE ON THE EASTERN FRONT 1941–1945

RARE PHOTOGRAPHS FROM WARTIME ARCHIVES

Ian Baxter

Pen & Sword
MILITARY

First published in Great Britain in 2021 by
PEN & SWORD MILITARY
an imprint of
Pen & Sword Books Ltd
47 Church Street
Barnsley
South Yorkshire
S70 2AS

ISBN 978-1-52676-807-0

A CIP catalogue record for this book is available from the British Library.

Typeset by Concept, Huddersfield, West Yorkshire HD4 5JL
Printed and bound in England by CPI Group (UK) Ltd, Croydon CR0 4YY

FSC www.fsc.org MIX Paper from responsible sources FSC® C013604

Pen & Sword Books Limited incorporates the imprints of Atlas, Archaeology, Aviation, Discovery, Family History, Fiction, History, Maritime, Military, Military Classics, Politics, Select, Transport, True Crime, Air World, Frontline Publishing, Leo Cooper, Remember When, Seaforth Publishing, The Praetorian Press, Wharncliffe Local History, Wharncliffe Transport, Wharncliffe True Crime and White Owl.

For a complete list of Pen & Sword titles please contact
PEN & SWORD BOOKS LIMITED
47 Church Street, Barnsley, South Yorkshire S70 2AS, England
E-mail: enquiries@pen-and-sword.co.uk
Website: www.pen-and-sword.co.uk

Contents

About the Author

Ian Baxter is a military historian who specialises in German twentieth-century military history. He has written more than fifty books including *Poland – The Eighteen Day Victory March, Panzers In North Africa, The Ardennes Offensive, The Western Campaign, The 12th SS Panzer-Division Hitlerjugend, The Waffen-SS on the Western Front, The Waffen-SS on the Eastern Front, The Red Army at Stalingrad, Elite German Forces of World War II, Armoured Warfare, German Tanks of War, Blitzkrieg, Panzer-Divisions at War, Hitler's Panzers, German Armoured Vehicles of World War Two, Last Two Years of the Waffen-SS at War, German Soldier Uniforms and Insignia, German Guns of the Third Reich, Defeat to Retreat: The Last Years of the German Army At War 1943–45, Operation Bagration the Destruction of Army Group Centre, German Guns of the Third Reich, Rommel and the Afrika Korps, U-Boat War*, and most recently *The Sixth Army and the Road to Stalingrad*. He has written over a hundred articles including 'Last days of Hitler', 'Wolf's Lair', 'The Story of the V1 and V2 Rocket Programme', 'Secret Aircraft of World War Two', 'Rommel at Tobruk', 'Hitler's War With his Generals', 'Secret British Plans to Assassinate Hitler', 'The SS at Arnhem', 'Hitlerjugend', 'Battle of Caen 1944', 'Gebirgsjäger at War', 'Panzer Crews', 'Hitlerjugend Guerrillas', 'Last Battles in the East', 'The Battle of Berlin', and many more. He has also reviewed numerous military studies for publication, supplied thousands of photographs and important documents to various publishers and film production companies worldwide, and lectures to various schools, colleges and universities throughout the United Kingdom and the Republic of Ireland.

Introduction

Prelude to Winter Operations

When the German soldier ventured into Russia as Operation Barbarossa was unleashed, the Red Army were a complete enigma to him. He had very little information about the country which he was invading. He simply saw the Russians as a race of inferior Slavic people. The propaganda was that all Russians were living in poverty and its antiquated army was totally unprepared for war. The German soldiers were amazed by the immense forests, the huge expanses of marshland, and the many rivers that were continuously flooding. There were few roads and those that they came across were in a terrible state of repair.

In spite of this, the Russian Army was overwhelmed by the Wehrmacht's furious onslaught, and as the first phase of the attack on Moscow began at the end of September 1941 – Operation Typhoon – German commanders were confident that victory would soon come. However, by early October the weather began to change. Cold driving rain fell on the troops and the roads and fields around Moscow became boggy swamps and virtually impassable.

Moreover, by the time Army Group Centre assembled to capture the Russian capital, it had lost 35,000 men, excluding the sick and injured. Some 240 tanks and heavy artillery pieces and 800 other vehicles had either developed mechanical problems or been destroyed. Most vehicles had not fallen to enemy fire but were lost to the muddy terrain. Supplies were becoming dangerously low, and fuel and ammunition were hardly adequate for the forthcoming attack.

(**Opposite, above**) The opening phase of Operation Barbarossa, the invasion of Russia, which was launched on 22 June 1941. This photograph shows a multitude of vehicles including the Pz.Kpfw.I, II and IV advancing along a road supported by a motorcyclist and infantry. The bulk of an infantry division rode in trucks, cars, wagons, and carts or on horses, bicycles and motorcycles, but its rifle companies walked.

(**Above**) During the summer of 1941 and what appears to be a signal unit, with its equipment stowed in brown leather cases loaded on pack mules, crosses a minefield with a cleared lane marked by white tape. Mules were often used by the Gebirgsjäger (mountain troops).

(**Opposite, below**) Infantry are seen here clambering into an Sd.Kfz.251 halftrack as another soldier runs to catch up the column in an attempt to climb into the vehicle as well. The halftrack offered infantry armoured protection and mobility until they were close enough to attack enemy positions on foot. The use of motorized infantry was an example of rapid tactical deployment that would change the way that battles were fought forever. These troops had been trained always to be on the move, and during an attack often supported by advancing armour, protecting their flanks and being dropped in the middle of a battle to mop up a bewildered and shocked foe.

(**Opposite, above**) In October 1941 the rains came in Russia. The mud produced from a few hours of rain was enough to turn a relatively typical Russian road into a quagmire. Here soldiers struggle with their motorcycle combination through a road section churned into mud.

(**Opposite, below**) Another photo showing infantry struggling through mud with their BMW R61 or R66 motorcycle combination. Note the white tactical marking on the front of the sidecar, which identifies the unit as the staff of a pioneer battalion.

(**Above**) A motorcycle rifle unit or Kradschützen, probably in late September or early October 1941, watches as a crew push-starts their motorcycle combination along a typical road churned up by continuous traffic. These units were employed basically for reconnaissance, screening, flank security, and other similar missions. One of the hazards of travelling by motorcycle, especially in the Soviet Union, was the lack of good-quality roads. Motorcyclists who decided to avoid the roads and travel cross-country often regretted their choice. The casualty rate among motorcyclists was high.

(**Above**) A converted Sd.Kfz.221 radio car drives through a Russian village following a downpour. Note the 'Y' insignia painted in yellow, indicating it belongs to the 7th Panzer Division. This retrofitted frame antenna looks distorted, indicating hard service.

(**Opposite, above**) A civilian vehicle has been commandeered for the advance through Russia and can be seen accompanying an infantry column through a muddy village in October 1941. Note the vehicle on the right with the tactical symbol E painted in yellow on the back. This denotes that it belongs to the 3rd Panzer Division. The 3rd operated initially on the central sector of the advance but was redirected south to participate in the Battle of Kiev. From there it participated in the Battle of Moscow, advancing towards Tula. With the Soviet counterattacks in the winter of 1941/2 the division acted as a stand-by emergency force until operations resumed in the spring.

(**Opposite, below**) A column of armoured vehicles, part of Army Group Centre, during operations in October 1941. Here units are facing the horrors of mud in the Orel sector. In western Russia the roads had not been constructed to carry vast amounts of heavy traffic. This road is on the Roslavl highway and has been reduced to a mud track. In some parts of the advance units found the mud around 1 metre deep.

(**Above**) Along a muddy road and a support vehicle has become stuck in the quagmire. A Raupenschlepper Ost or Caterpillar Tractor East, or RSO halftrack, is about to pull the vehicle out. This fully tracked vehicle was brought to the front in response to the poor performance of wheeled and half-tracked vehicles in the mud and snow during the Wehrmacht's first autumn and winter in Russia.

(**Opposite, above**) A typical scene on the Ostfront in Army Group Centre. A support vehicle more than likely carrying supplies has become stuck in the mud and soldiers are trying to relieve its rear wheels from the mire. German commanders observed with considerable alarm how roads simply vanished in just a few hours of rain, and soon realized how dependent they were on the few all-weather roads that had been built in Western Russia.

(**Opposite, below**) Units of the Das Reich Division during its drive on the central front in the autumn of 1941 with Guderian's Panzergruppe. Note how heavy traffic has turned the road into a wet and boggy quagmire. Pioneers appear to be trying to make good parts of the road.

G

Chapter One

The First Winter 1941/42

The Road to Disaster

In most areas the weather had brought whole columns of wheeled vehicles to a standstill. Horses, the main mode of transport, of which there were some 800,000 on the Eastern Front in 1941, died from heart strain as soldiers frantically tried to pull them through the mud. Bogged-down units became sitting targets.

The main rainy season lasted for approximately three to four weeks. Commanders began drawing up plans to regulate the flow of traffic. Pioneers were sent ahead of the main columns to try to improve the roads. In some areas only tracked vehicles were allowed to advance. Transport vehicles were authorised to travel alongside the tracked vehicles, but using a parallel track to the main road. Commanders were becoming concerned about the lack of supplies.

After a week the weather improved slightly and on 12 October 3rd Panzer Army reported it had captured Volokolamsk. Following heavy fighting, advanced elements cut the Kalinin–Klin highway 40 miles north of Moscow.

However, during the last two weeks of October, weather conditions became much worse and enemy resistance grew. A combination of heavy rain, snow showers, and enveloping mists made movement almost impossible for the German units. Slowly the movement of the Panzers halted as the freeze set in.

Elsewhere along the front, General Erich von Manstein had assigned missions to overrun the Crimea and take Rostov. Initially the advance went well, advancing towards Sevastopol and beginning to secure the Donets river line. Since the summer the 6th Army had had considerable success in the area. But in October they too began to suffer from the rains.

By the end of October it was clear to the Germans that the war would not be won that year as the High Command had initially predicted. It was also apparent that their vehicles, equipment and clothing were inferior to those of the Russian army.

To keep warm, soldiers had to wear every piece of clothing, even the clothing of the dead of both sides: overcoats, fur hats and boots, particularly the excellent Russian felt boots. Over time the German leather boot retained the damp, and constant exposure to snow and wet caused them to fall apart. Socks became wet and caused frostbite. Soldiers lined their boots with straw or paper, if they could find those materials.

Another problem was camouflage. Soldiers carried white sheets and draped them over their steel helmets, secured by the helmet's rubber ring. The sheet was then normally wrapped around the wearer's head and secured by a pin or metal hook beneath the chin. The rest of the sheet was draped around the arms and upper body and fastened again by another single pin or metal hook on the front. Sometimes they did not fasten the sheet as it did not allow the wearer to move freely enough, but this compromised camouflage effectiveness. It also limited easy access to equipment, especially under combat conditions.

German soldiers also used the snow shirt. Pulled over the head, it was rather tight-fitting. It had no collar, and long sleeves. The snow shirt had been purposely made long with the shirttails reaching down to the ankles. They were very popular during the first winter on the Eastern Front. The soldier not only blended well with the local terrain, but was able to move more freely than with the snow sheet. The wearer's personal equipment too was worn outside it.

During this time soldiers were also issued with the snow overall, very similar in design to the snow shirt. This item of clothing was not tight fitting; it was a shapeless long overall garment, buttoned right down the front. It had a deep collar, and for the first time it had an attached hood and long sleeves. The overall was generally liked among the soldiers for concealment, but it soon proved impractical as it tended to restrict the wearer.

But supplies of these items were limited, and many soldiers were stuck with their Standard Army Greatcoat. For these men, it was a matter of trying to keep warm and staying alive. After a patrol or fighting, the soldier returned to his primitive dugout numb and cold. In their dugouts they had little stoves fuelled with methylated spirit. Unable to undress due to the cold, the soldier would wear every piece of his clothing all the time, including his greatcoat.

Following his daily brief the soldier would either go on patrol through waist deep snow, defend a particular line, or undertake a local attack against an enemy position. Lines consisted of shallow trenches and simple shelters, and often to be driven out of these shelters meant death. Across the entire German front in late 1941, most units had frozen into immobility.

(**Opposite, above**) A motorcyclist has problems with his machine due to the extremely muddy conditions. He is wearing the standard waterproof coat, which has a collar faced in field-grey wool and two large pockets in the front and side, each with a large button-down pocket flap. He is armed with a 7.92mm Kar 98k Mauser bolt-action rifle.

(**Opposite, below**) A pair of 2cm FlaK30 Sd.Kfz.10/4 halftracks are part of column that is struggling along a muddy road. Note the leading halftrack, behind the horse and cart, hauling an Sd.Ah.51 trailer. Of particular interest is the motorcyclist stuck in the mud and being prepared to be towed along the road by a horse.

(**Above**) Infantrymen watch as a support vehicle hauling a trailer of supplies struggles through the mud. By the end of October much of the front in Army Group Centre and North had been reduced to a painful crawl as vehicles and animals struggled through endless mud.

(**Opposite, above**) A host of civilian wheeled transport was used by the Wehrmacht during the invasion of the Soviet Union. They were helpful for supplying the front and aiding the advance, but along inadequate roads, across fields and in mud and snow they proved a hindrance. Here infantrymen are seen trying to free a stuck civilian vehicle.

(**Opposite, below**) One of the best ways to get from one place to another was to hitch a lift on a Panzer. Here soldiers can be seen mounted on a Pz.Kpfw.38(t) in autumn in Russia.

From a defensive position an infantryman can be seen wearing the early style greatcoat with M1935 steel helmet. He is preparing a concentration charge, which was primarily used as an anti-tank weapon or for knocking out bunkers. The charge was made by securing six stick grenade heads with detonators removed around the central stick grenade. The weapon could cause a tremendous blast.

A group of troops on the Eastern Front in the first winter in Russia in 1941. They all wear the standard pattern army field-grey greatcoat with dark blue-green collar worn with a woollen toque, and mittens. They can be seen drinking some hot fluid from an M1938 field cap.

A column of Pz.Kpfw.38(t)s on a snowy road. By this stage of the war the Russian army was beginning to fight back and the light tanks began to meet significant numbers of new T-34 and KV-1 tanks. The Pz.Kpfw.38(t) was no match for this new superior enemy armour, and losses grew to staggering proportions.

Troops marching through the snow in late 1941. The soldier leading the march is wearing a white cotton blanket crudely tied around his tunic. This was an early attempt by troops at snow camouflage. Behind, the men wear a mixture of camouflage clothing including the two-piece snowsuit, snow shirts, and snow overalls.

Soldiers of the Gebirgsjäger trudge along a road in the rain while operating on the southern sector of the Eastern Front. The soldiers are wearing the waterproof camouflaged cape or Zeltbahn. The Zeltbahn was first issued in 1931 and was carried by each German soldier as part of his personal equipment. It could be worn as a poncho over the field equipment, and it could also be worn buttoned up under the equipment as a form of camouflage.

Freezing German troops are attempting to protect themselves from the snow with their Zeltbahn. The Zeltbahn was not considered a winter garment and although it protected the wearer from the snow showers it did not keep the wearer warm. It appears that these soldiers are not even wearing their greatcoats.

Infantrymen halt in their advance in the snow and pose for the camera. A horse can be seen towing a sled full of supplies. During Operation Typhoon, in spite of the terrible arctic conditions, the German army relied heavily on the horse for motive power. Sometimes thousands were lost each day in combat or due to extreme weather conditions.

Waffen-SS soldiers of the Das Reich Division. This photograph shows how unprepared these troops were for winter combat. Most wear their standard army issue greatcoat. One is seen wearing the woollen toque, a popular winter item. Scarves were sometimes worn with the toque. Two soldiers are still wearing their summer Waffen-SS camouflage smocks.

A Pz.Kpfw.38(t) has halted on a snowy road. At this stage of the war the ever increasing demand to replenish the Panzerwaffe with heavier Panzers was eventually to see the relegation of the 38(t) to second-line duties and be converted into tank hunters.

A Pz.Kpfw.II Ausf.F during winter operations on the Ost Front. This variant is identified by the straight superstructure front plate, the retention of the five road-wheels with spring bundles for the suspension, the return rollers, track links with pairs of edge-mounted guide horns, drive sprockets and the later style idler wheel.

(**Above**) In a snow-covered forest is a Waffen-SS signalman operating a portable radio. This device was the standard radio used at battalion and regimental level. These radios were carried by a soldier on a specially designed backpack frame, and when connected to each other (upper and lower valves) via special cables, could be used on the march.

(**Opposite, above**) An artillery crew all wearing toques and the standard army greatcoat can be seen between a 15cm artillery gun on tow and a Volkswagen Type 82 personnel carrier. The supplies on the sled are probably going to be hauled by a horse. This photograph was taken during the first winter on the Eastern Front in late 1941.

(**Opposite, below**) Infantry march along a road during 'Typhoon'. These soldiers are equipped with the web battle-pack carrier to which was attached their mess kit, shelter cape, and other important equipment. All the men wear the toque, a sleeve-like wool tube designed to be pulled over the head to protect the wearer's neck and parts of the face from the bitter cold. Occasionally two or even three toques were worn for extra insulation, along with scarves.

(**Above**) Two soldiers more than likely on guard duty. Both wear the standard army field greatcoat with woollen toque beneath their M1938 field cap.

(**Opposite, above**) An attempt has been made to whitewash this Pz.Kpfw.38(t), which is advancing across a snowy road with a column of horse-drawn infantry moving in a different direction. The placement of the Notek blackout driving headlamp on the glacis of the tank identifies this as being an Ausf.G variant. A road wheel can be stored on the bow and is acting as a stowage tray for cables and other gear.

(**Opposite, below**) The first winter on the Eastern Front and troops use animals to pull sleds along a road during Army Group Centre's drive on Moscow. The soldiers are wearing the standard issue greatcoat with toque and M1938 field cap. The German army lacked the provisions necessary to sustain their forces for a winter war and many thousands got frostbite and other ailments caused by the cold.

(**Opposite, above**) Two soldiers stand next to their partly whitewashed vehicle. This crew have covered the front of the radiator grill to prevent freezing. Straw has also been applied over the sides of the engine cover.

(**Opposite, below**) Wehrmacht troops with their 'goulash wagons' on board flat bed railway cars during operations in November 1941. Note troops of the Totenkopf Division queuing for their food. It is apparent in this photograph that there is a lack of proper winter clothing.

(**Above**) Two Waffen-SS soldiers can be seen in a dugout inside a forest. The soldier on the left still wears his summer camouflage tunic while his comrade wears the standard greatcoat complete with toque. Over the coming weeks soldiers would be compelled to fight against an enemy who intended to deny them any shelter.

An MG34 heavy machine-gun crew await orders to move forward. The man behind the gunner carries the weapons tripod. Most of the crew are seen wearing the familiar winter wool helmet toque. An infantry battalion's machine-gun company had three platoons of four heavy machine guns each, plus an 8cm mortar platoon.

To blend in with the local terrain this SS Squad Leader wears a piece of crude white sheeting both wrapped around his tunic and on his M35 steel grey slate helmet. By November large batches of winter garments were hastily dispatched to the front-line combat troops.

Brücke
16to

(**Opposite, above**) A photograph taken during the preparation of a whitewashed 21cm Mrs18 Mörser opening fire against an enemy target. These weapons were designed to fire projectiles at higher than normal angles of elevation for long range. They could inflict considerable damage on enemy lines and were used extensively on the Ostfront to destroy fortifications, bunker systems and any other enemy defensive position.

(**Opposite, below**) A StuG.III is about to cross a bridge bound for the front lines. For the invasion of Russia German factories were able to supply 548 StuG.III vehicles. The StuG had a crew of four and came equipped with a 7.5cm KwK 37 L/24 gun capable of traversing 12.5 degrees left and right. With the vehicle's low silhouette, it provided sterling service both in defence and offence. Note the infantryman standing on his prime mover that has evidently fallen off the bridge and lies on its side.

(**Above**) A halted column in the snow and members of a motorcycle unit with sidecar combination can be seen on a road. They are both wearing the double-breasted rubberised motorcycle coat with woollen toque. In summer operations motorcycle units were flexible and fast moving, especially along the more open roads. The motorcycle was used in both combat and reconnaissance roles. Each infantry and Panzer division incorporated hundreds of motorcycles which were distributed among the Panzer and rifle regiments, flak detachments, artillery regiments, supply units, signals and reconnaissance.

(**Above**) A soldier poses for the camera standing beside a halftrack with a Russian peasant infant during operations on the road to Moscow. The winter had caused the front to stagnate until the spring thaw of 1942, delaying the conquest of Russia by months.

(**Opposite, above**) Pioneers on board a prime mover towing what appears to be part of a bridging section. The halftrack was undoubtedly the workhorse on the Eastern Front. Its effective towing capability ensured that troops and ordnance often got through when they otherwise wouldn't have.

(**Opposite, below**) Infantry pose for the camera in front of their stationary prime movers. They wear the standard army greatcoat and M1938 field cap. Under the greatcoat they are more than likely wearing the M1936 field service uniform tucked into the traditional long shaft leather marching boots. Their winter clothing during this period consisted of woollen toques worn under the M1935 steel helmet, and thick woollen gloves. They would wear over the greatcoat the usual rifleman's equipment and weapons including the leather belt and ammunition pouches.

10

A soldier at a lookout post peers through a pair of 6 × 30 Sf.14Z Scherenfernrohr (scissor binoculars) which were nicknamed 'donkey ears'. They were used to estimate ranges. Observation posts like this were normally located well forward of the infantry they supported, and it was essential that they were well dug in and concealed.

A typical scene during the German advance during the first winter. Here soldiers using rope are attempting to pull a supply vehicle across the snow. It must have been hard work.

(**Opposite, above**) Infantry stand next to their wheeled vehicle on one of the many pieces of marshland that covered western Russian. Pine logs have been laid across the boggy swamps.

(**Opposite, below**) An infantryman lies across a vehicle's fender sleeping, obviously to keep warm. The driver can also be seen sleeping.

(**Above**) There were more than 800,000 horses on the Eastern Front in 1941, and in the winter some 8,000 a day were being killed by enemy fire, the extreme arctic temperatures and over-exertion. Here a group of soldiers tend to a horse that has clearly overexerted itself trying to pull a cart through the snow and mud. Most of the troops wear the standard pattern army field-grey greatcoat with dark blue-green collar. An officer is also wearing the army pattern field-grey greatcoat, which is identical to those worn by other ranks except for the reinforced leather patches to the shoulders indicating his rank, and the officers' field cap.

(**Opposite, above**) Soldiers stand in front of a support vehicle. Only one of the troops is wearing the new improvised snow garment as much of the winter supplies that were being rushed to the front were slow to arrive. The army greatcoat with black wool toque and wool mittens was still the standard winter kit even in December when temperatures plummeted to –50°C.

(**Opposite, below**) Infantry can be seen marching through the snow wearing what were called Schnee-Tarnung Uberzug or snow coveralls. This was another form of early-period winter white snow camouflage clothing which comprised a long coverall which covered the entire service uniform and was designed to reach the wearer's ankles. It had buttons right down the front, a deep collar, an attached hood and long sleeves.

(**Above**) Troops marching through the snow wearing snow coveralls. Note that the black infantryman's leather belt and personal equipment is being worn attached around the outside the garment to allow better access.

A group of soldiers, mostly with their gas mask canisters slung round to the front of their chests, pose in front of a Pz.Kpfw.II in the winter. The tank cannot be identified other than part of its tactical number painted in yellow on its turret side showing '10'. Note that the vehicle still retains its factory grey as most tanks during this early period never had white camouflage wash. The two tank men are still wearing the old style black panzer beret, which would be phased out completely by the end of the year.

Chapter Two

The Second Winter 1942/43

By early 1942 the Russian offensive had begun to falter and the front had stagnated. This was a welcome relief to the battle-weary German army. Fortunately for the exhausted Panzer crews and supporting units no mobile operations had been planned for the winter. Most of the Panzer divisions were pulled out of their dormant defensive positions and transferred to France, to rest, reorganize and retrain.

Back in Germany, production of tanks increased. To overcome the mammoth task of defeating the Red Army more Panzer divisions were raised, and motorized divisions were converted into Panzergrenadier divisions.

Manufacturers were designing more practical winter garments for the infantry. One such item was the two-piece snowsuit. Another was the single-piece snow overall, which became one of the most efficient forms of winter wear they ever produced. A number of other winter items were put into service, but their quality varied.

When the spring thaw arrived in March 1942, the German soldier could be seen wearing a host of new summer and winter camouflage uniforms, newly designed steel helmets and field caps. Even the Panzer uniforms were being replaced.

The objective of summer 1942 was to take Stalingrad. But in May not all of the divisions were ready. Some units were not back to strength after their losses of the previous winter. They were sent to Army Group North or Army Group Centre. Army Group South consisted of only the best-equipped forces. It seemed all Germany's hopes and successes hinged on this operation.

The steppes were good tank country but they lacked drinking water and many soldiers suffered as a result. Yet despite the hardships, each man was determined to fulfil his duty, reach the Volga, and capture the city. The Operation – Fall Blau – was supposed to deprive the Red Army of the resources necessary to continue the war.

Though the offensive initially went well, with advanced forces reaching the Don in July, enemy resistance grew and commanders became concerned that another winter on the Eastern Front would have to be endured.

During the summer, High Command had produced a handbook on winter warfare which would be later issued to the troops. At 372 pages, including many drawings and diagrams, the *Taschenbuch für den Winterkrieg* (or *Paperback for the Winter War*) dealt with the building of various types of shelter, including igloos. It covered the building of stoves and log fires. It gave instruction on the use of sleds, which were an effective way to transport food rations, ammunition and equipment in the snow. It explained how ski troops could advance rapidly through the snow and use sleds to move wounded comrades. There were pages devoted to food, animal care, the maintenance of vehicles, and the best ways to camouflage tanks in the snow. It admitted that the supply of clothing for the 1941 winter had not been adequate, but went on to reassure the reader that this would be rectified in the future.

The handbook also emphasised the advantages of winter warfare, for example that it was particularly easy to dig trenches, shelters, and build walls of snow as wind breakers. It advised soldiers to use forests, where snow would lie less deeply, and that troops follow tank tracks in the snow as this would make the infantry less traceable to the enemy.

Towards the end of 1942, the infantry and panzer divisions of Army Group South were embroiled in a bitter and bloody battle. Around the smouldering city of Stalingrad troops were struggling through deep snow and freezing temperatures. By 24 November, 30,000 Rumanian soldiers had capitulated. Within days the Russians had surrounded the German 6th Army, and cut off their supply lines and any chance of retreat they might have hoped for.

Von Manstein assembled his forces for a relief attempt on Stalingrad: Operation Winter Storm. At first his panzers made good progress over the light snow, but they soon came up against fierce resistance and became bogged down. Eventually they ground to a halt in the snow, leaving 250,000 German troops imprisoned between Stalingrad and the bend of the Don.

(**Opposite, above**) Gebirgsjäger ski-troops wearing their distinctive two-piece snowsuits during reconnaissance operations. The distances over which the soldiers had to travel were immense. Although these mountain forces sustained heavy casualties during the winter of 1941, they grimly held the line, and by early 1942 a stalemate with the Russians had developed. Before spring only minor skirmishes continued as both sides rebuilt their strength.

(**Opposite, below**) Inside a bunker and a heavy MG34 machine gunner can be seen wearing his animal skin during a fire action. The machine gun is mounted on the sustained-fire mount. Each infantry battalion contained an MG Company, which fielded eight MG34 heavy machine-guns on the sustained-fire mount.

A mortar crew have a cigarette break during a lull in the fighting. They are all wearing the two-piece snowsuit and one crewman has received an application of whitewash to his steel helmet. Those that survived the ordeal of the Russian winter got a medal to prove that they had been there. Troops nicknamed the decoration the 'Frozen Meat Medal'.

Photographed the moment an 8cm sGrW 34 mortar is fired against an enemy target. The weapon and crew blend well with the local terrain. Each battalion fielded some six of these excellent 8cm sGrW 34 mortars, which could fire fifteen projectiles mortar a minute to a range of 2,625 yards.

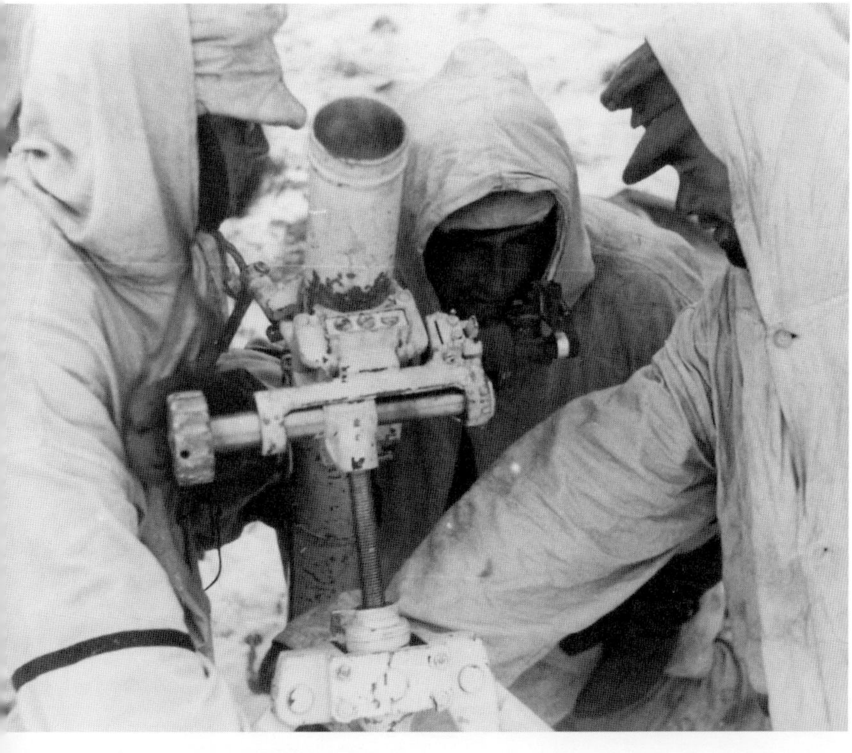

A Gebirgsjäger mortar crew preparing to fire their weapon. The men are all wearing the two-piece winter suit. Note the soldier on the right with his jacket buttoned up displaying the white metal buttons. The mountain troops used the mortar extensively. The weapon was light, easy to carry, and gave the infantryman his own portable artillery support. But it required training to use; even experienced mortar crews could take several rounds to achieve just one successful hit on target.

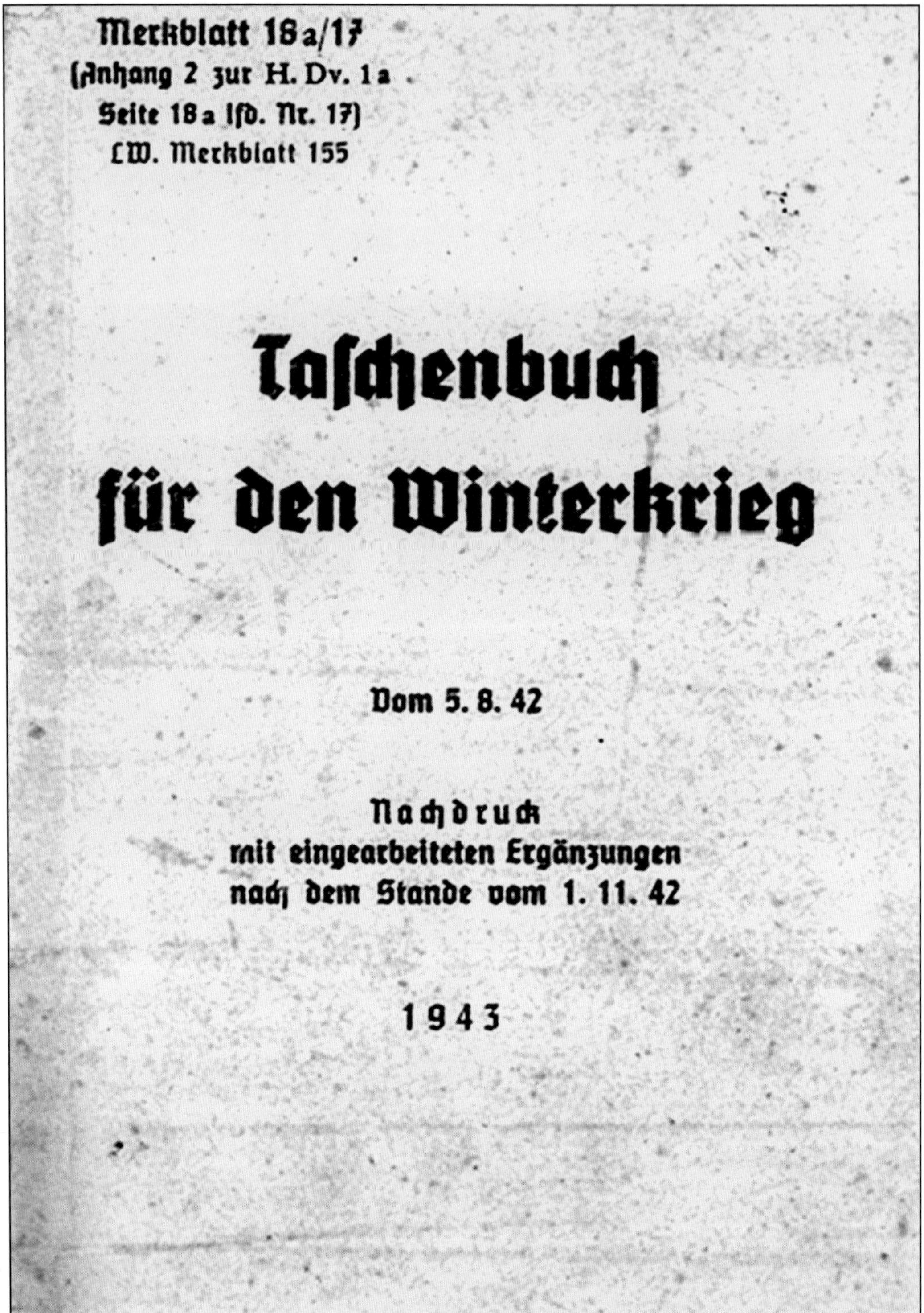

Merkblatt 18a/17
(Anhang 2 zur H. Dv. 1a
Seite 18a lfd. Nr. 17)
LW. Merkblatt 155

Taschenbuch
für den Winterkrieg

Vom 5. 8. 42

Nachdruck
mit eingearbeiteten Ergänzungen
nach dem Stande vom 1. 11. 42

1943

After the harsh winter of 1941/2, High Command produced the *Taschenbuch für den Winterkrieg* (*Paperback for the Winter War*). It was distributed down to infantry level.

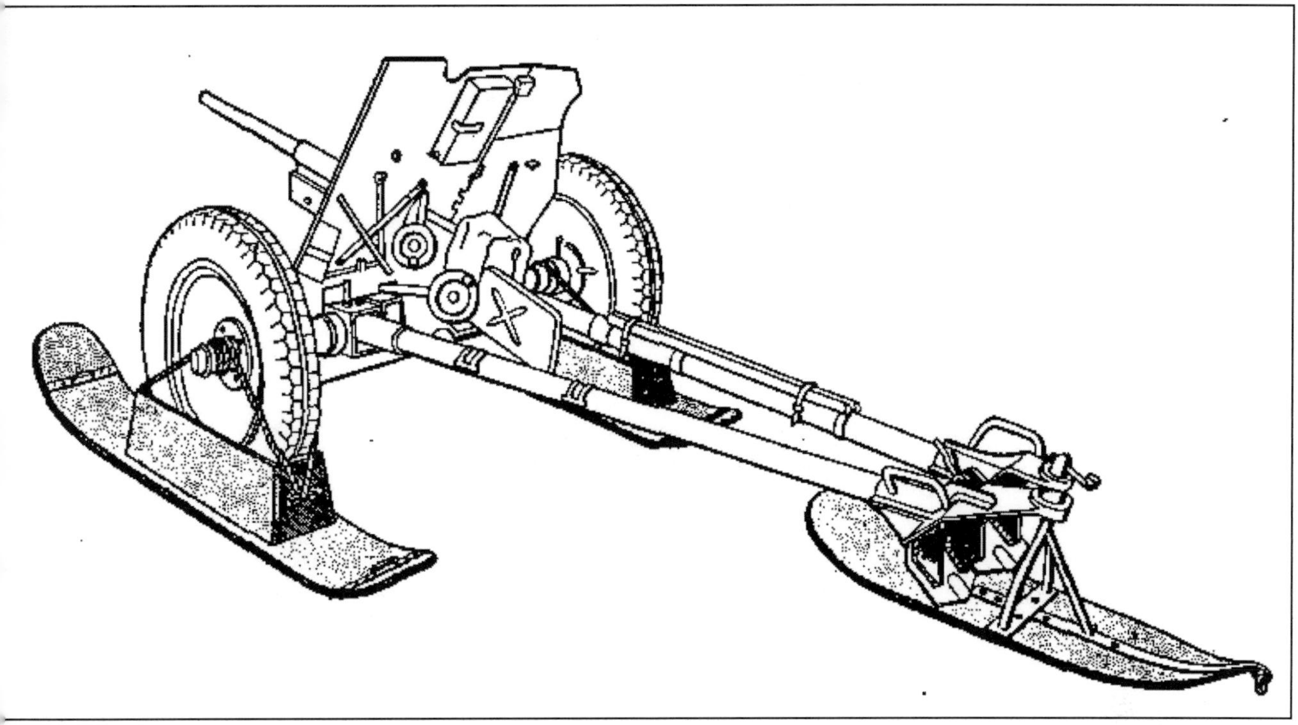

The chapter headed 'Skis, Snowshoes, and Snow' outlines mobility in winter warfare. It covers both troops and vehicles. It stresses the importance of mobility of anti-tank weapons in winter. This figure shows a PaK35/36 anti-tank gun with ski runners attached.

A whitewashed 7.5cm PaK40 being hauled by a Steyr-built RSO tractor. As described by the winter warfare handbook, it has sled-like skids under each wheel.

This section deals with patrols in the snow and reduction of tracks using the formation outlined in the figure drawing. It reads: Functions of the trail detail. (1) The leading pair cuts the first track; (2) the second pair clears the curves; (3) the squad leader maintains the direction of march; (4) this pair removes obstacles; (5) these men cut a third track (triple ski trail) for light sleds; (6) this pair levels the trail; (7) these men post road signs and improve the sled trail.

Ski troops out on patrol. They are all armed with the standard German infantry rifle, the Karbiner 98K bolt action rifle. The weapons, together with ammunition boxes, have been whitewashed.

During operations in southern Russia this Gebirgsjäger ski patrol wears the one-piece camouflage snow suit over their uniforms. Most men are carrying over their shoulder the Karbiner 98K carbine. Note the two soldiers with the ready-to-use 50-round MG34 machine gun belts draped around their necks.

Ski troops move across the snow. They are wearing the shapeless two-piece snow suit. To the right of the soldiers is a long column of troops hauling their supplies using a horse and sled. Movement like this was very risky during daylight hours as Red Army aircraft regularly attacked German formations out in the open.

A ski trooper clad in his white cape with hood and carrying a rucksack.

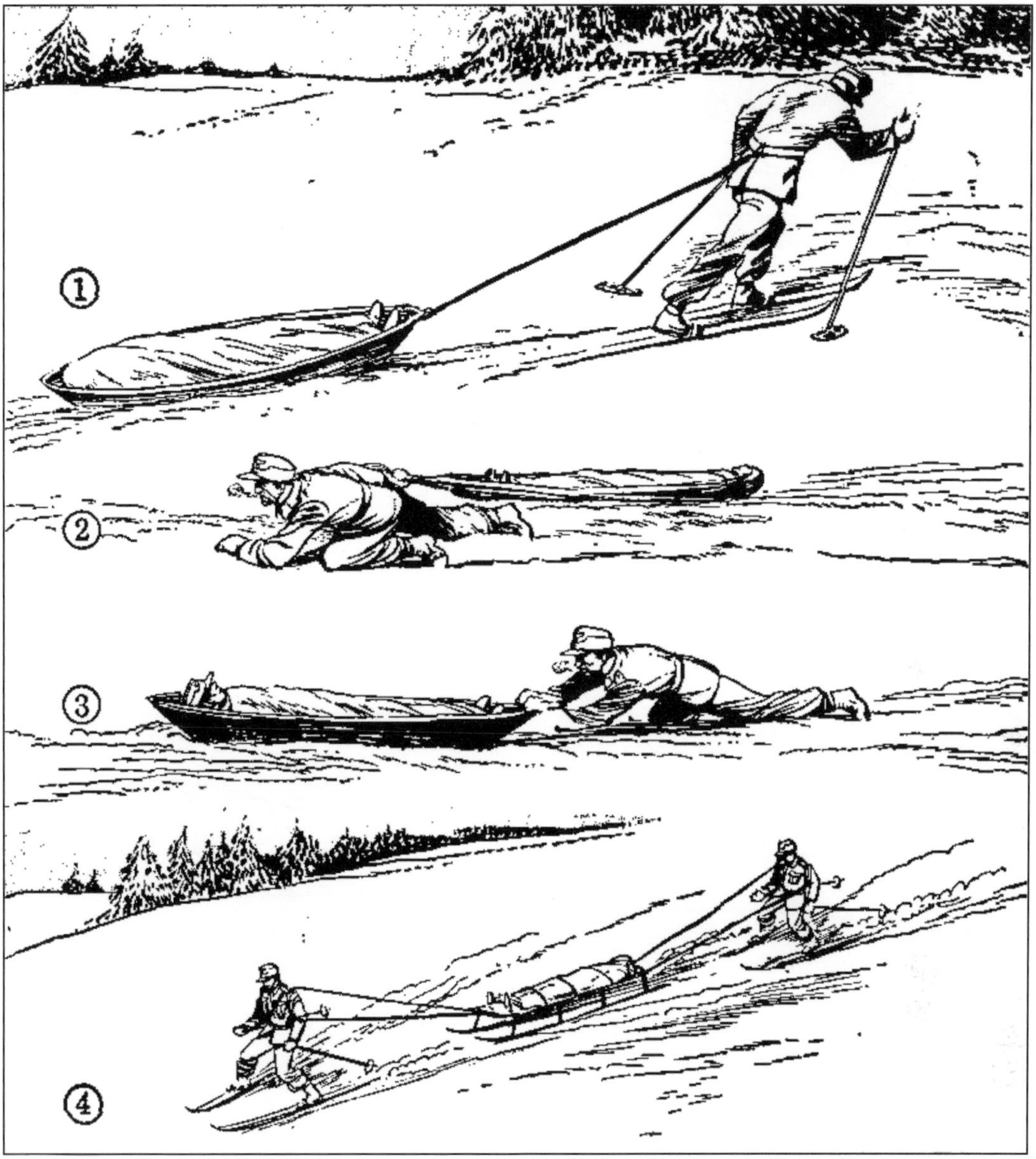

From 'Means of Evacuating Wounded' under 'Hand Sleds and Improvised Means': 'In some circumstances it may be necessary for two skiers to carry a man between them for short distances. The wounded man is placed on a shelter half, oblique to the direction of travel. The two bearers grasp the shelter half at either end and carry the wounded man between them, leaving their outside arm free for the ski pole. The bearers change places when their "carrying arm" gets tired. If only one bearer equipped with skis is available, the casualty is secured in the same manner. The skier pulls the wounded by means of a rope fastened to the point of the akja, or boat sled. A wounded man may be wrapped in a shelter half, secured with straps and belts, and dragged like a bundle. This method may be useful for evacuating a casualty from a field of fire into a defiladed area. Akjas, or boat sleds, are used in terrain under enemy observation or under direct fire. The wounded man is tied to the sled (which has been padded with woollen or fur blankets) with ropes or straps, and is pulled or pushed by the bearer while creeping. In easy terrain and under favourable snow conditions one skier is sufficient to haul a sled, but, as a rule, two men are employed to negotiate obstacles and slopes and to make greater speed.'

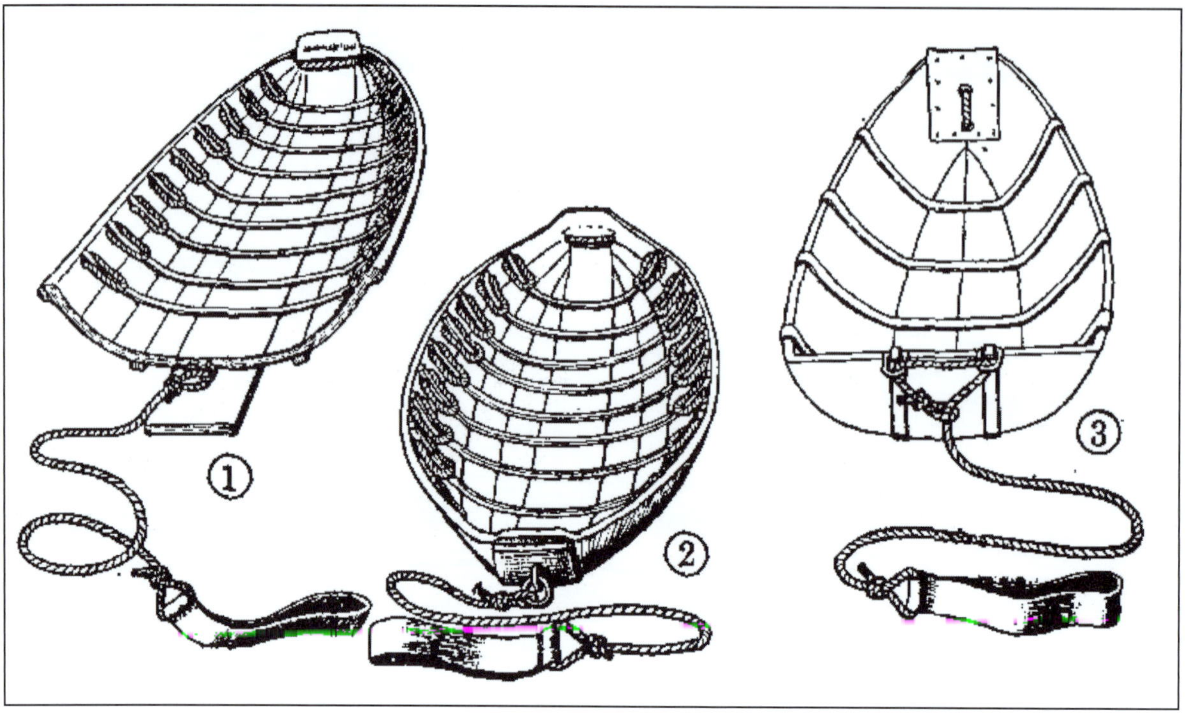

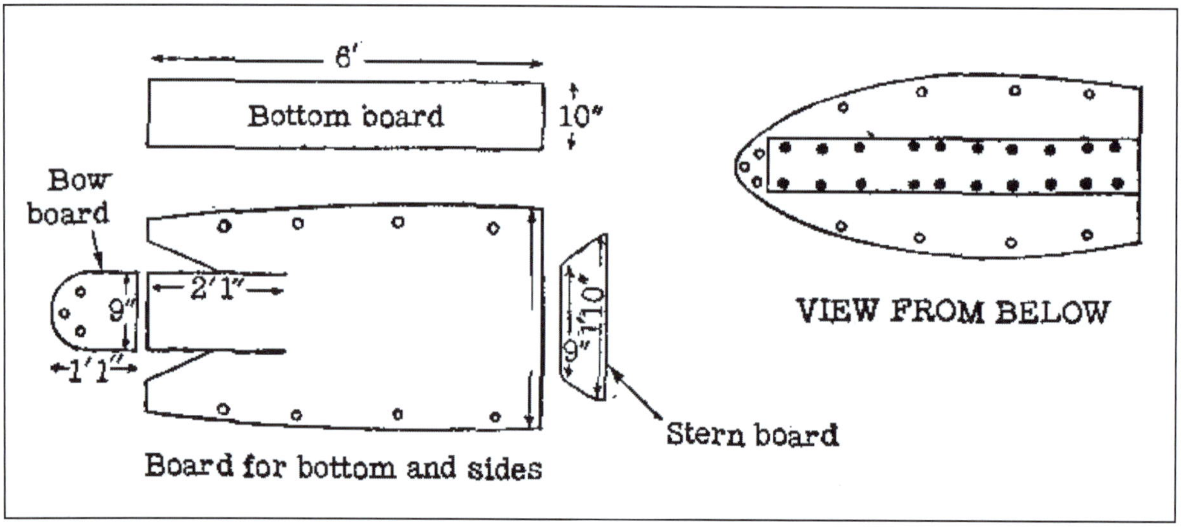

'Construction of Hand Sleds', (1) weapons toboggan (2) boat toboggan; (3) light toboggan: 'The light hand sled (Model Army Training School for Mountain Warfare – Modell Heereshochgebirgsschule) has proved very useful on the Eastern Front in snow of medium depth. It can be drawn by men, dogs, or horses and is made of old skis and other easily procurable material. No metal parts are used at the joints. The sled must be flexible and mobile, and the front part should be more lightly loaded than the rear. It has a weight of 9–11 pounds and can be drawn by one or more men, or by dogs. It can be used in trackless terrain. When drawn by skiers, the weight of the cargo should not be more than 80kg (176lbs); when drawn by dogs, not more than the total weight of the dogs'.

In 'Skis, Snowshoes, and Snow Vehicles' under 'Snow Sleds' this diagram shows the use of rescue toboggans, which is made of pinewood and is flat and boat-shaped: 'It is open at the rear, but a detachable board may be used as a stern piece. At the top of the inner walls, loops are provided for the ropes used to lash the load in place and to fasten the tarpaulin. It is used to transport light weapons (machine guns, mortars, light antitank rifles) and ammunition. The machine gun, light mortar, and light antitank rifle can be fired from the toboggan. There are two rings, one fastened to the front and one to the rear, for the towing and braking ropes. The toboggan can be hauled by one to three skiers, depending on the load. It can be used to transport signal equipment, ammunition, hand grenades, mines, food carriers, radio equipment, heavy mortars, flame-throwers, etc. It may also be used for the evacuation of wounded.'

Gebirgsjäger ski troops operating in northern Russia have halted in the snow and converse on their next movement. The *Taschenbuch für den Winterkrieg* noted, 'For winter warfare in the east and in the north, the soldier is equipped as much as possible with regulation as well as additional clothing, the issuance of which is based on experience of needs and available raw materials. Nevertheless it is necessary that the unit should try to overcome the cold independently by using winter clothing as effectively as possible and by devising additional expedients.'

(**Above**) Gebirgsjäger troops wear the two-piece snowsuit, whitewashed M1935 steel helmets and Karbiner 98K rifles while on patrol in northern Russia. A light 7.5cm Infantry Gun 18 can also be seen. The handbook says, 'For camouflage in snow, extensive use must be made of white clothing. For this purpose white camouflage cloaks and two-piece white uniforms are available. If the supply is insufficient for all combat troops, priority must be given to ski patrols, raiding parties on skis, sentries, and similar detachments. Camouflage is improved if the face is covered with a mask of transparent gauze fastened to the parka hood. White gloves, if available, are the best camouflage for the hands. The belt and equipment should be worn under the white cloak. The most effective camouflage for weapons, equipment, material, motor and other vehicles, tanks, sleds, and skis is white oil paint or whitewash, which is issued. To make improvised paints durable, the admixture of glue is recommended. If there is a shortage of paints, use chalk or lime dissolved in water.'

(**Opposite, above**) Two soldiers tucking into their rations are wearing the reversible snow suit. The man on the left wearing his M1935 camouflaged steel helmet has his padded winter garment white side out, while his comrade wearing an M1938 field cap with toque has it grey side out. The reversible grey side was officially manufactured in reed green, however factories seemed to have produced them in a darker steel-grey colour.

(**Opposite, below**) Soldiers, more than likely part of the Waffen-SS Polizei-Division, can be seen aiding an injured comrade. The infantryman on the right wears a snow coverall, while the soldier next to him wears the new winter reversible, grey side out. Three of the men are wearing captured Russian army Ushanka headgear with ear flaps.

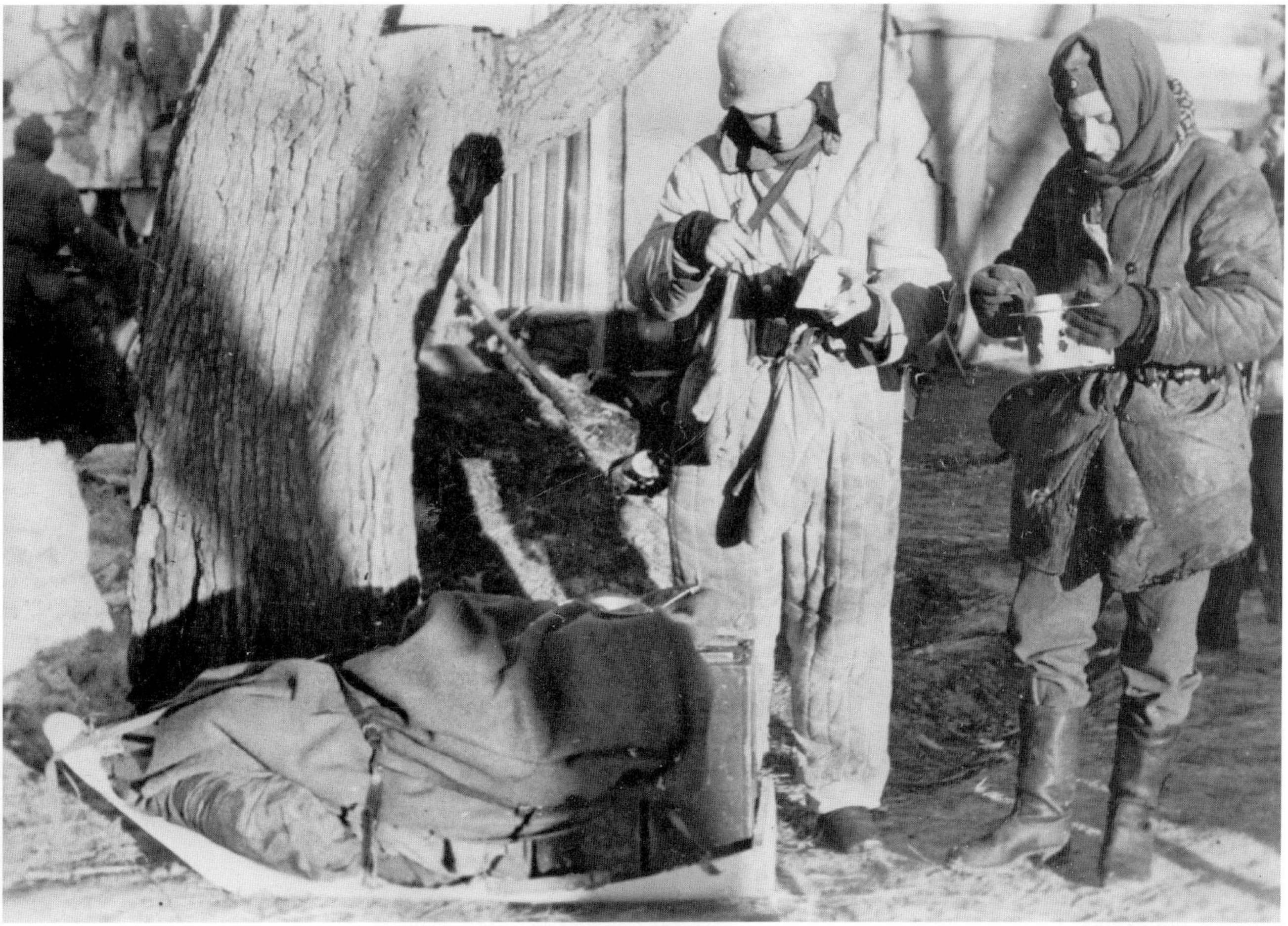
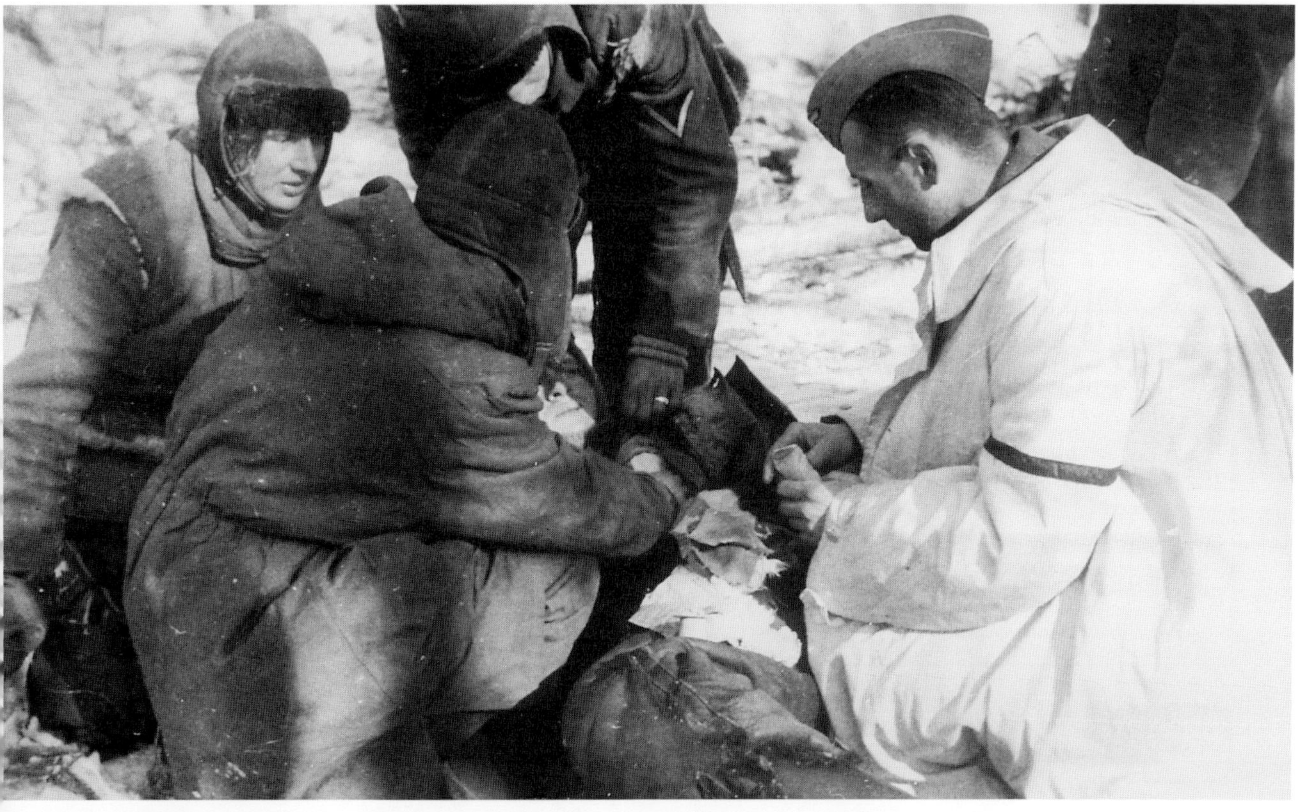

This diagram, headed 'Army sled', shows one method of transportation across the snow using animal draught. It describes that the structure is 'a one-piece vehicle that may be used to carry freight and personnel. For bulky loads such as crates wider than the carrying surface, the side and rear boards can be removed. The seat board in the front can be used as a driver's seat or to increase the height of the front wall, and other seat boards may be used similarly on the backboard. The shafts are two plain wooden poles, each with a ring for attaching them to the runners. On the rear cross bar above each runner is a towing hook to which toboggans or other light sleds can be attached. The army sled can be drawn by a single horse or a tandem.'

Under 'Runners and Sliding Troughs': 'In many instances runners have not proved effective, because they skid on slippery roads and do not have much carrying capacity in deep snow. They are, however, the only medium for the transportation of heavy material which cannot be loaded on sleds, particularly wheel guns must be brought into position. Runners have the advantage that they can be constructed by the troops, but a great disadvantage is that they do not fit into the tracks of sleds (usually they must be built to a greater width). Ski runners and snow or sled runners are issued as equipment of combat troops. The wheel pair of ski runners may also be used as gun supports during firing. The wheel and trail runners are issued with iron fittings but without wheel blocks; the latter must be constructed by the troops to fit the wheels. If the gun is to be hauled by troops, the runners must be provided with fittings for tow-ropes. The antitank guns (37–75mm), smoke-shell mortar, light infantry howitzer, and the recoilless gun can be carried on this type of runner. A set of snow or sled runners consists of two wheel runners and one trail runner. Both types are for hauling guns on roads with horses in tandem, and for supporting the gun while firing.'

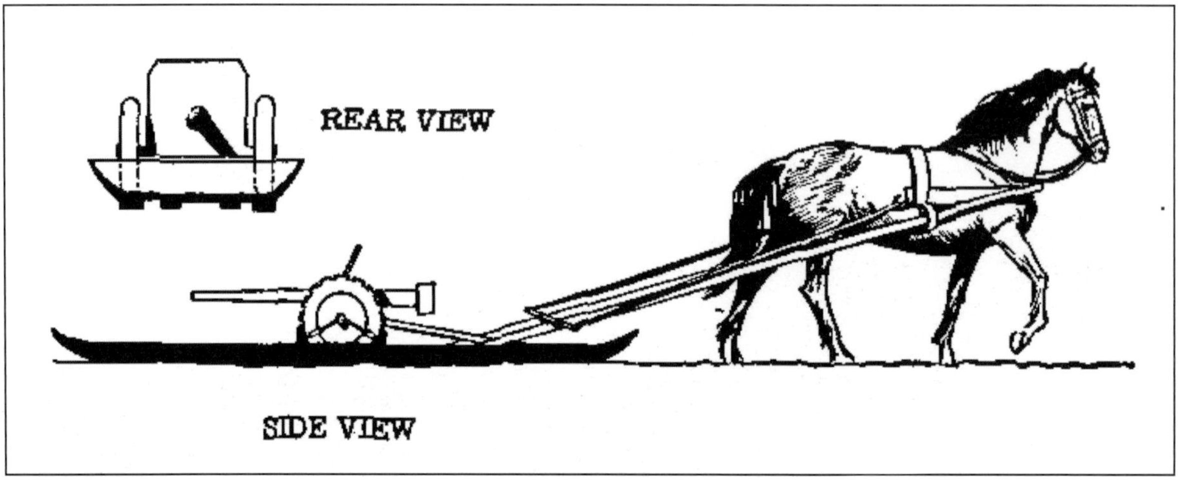

Ski troops of the Gebirgsjäger during winter operations in Army Group North. They are preparing to move out of a village with sleds full of supplies. The Gebirgsjäger were provided with ample supplies of winter clothing. Living in the snow could be difficult, but soldiers were taught that the snow could also serve as a friend.

A horse-drawn sled transporting an injured soldier to a field hospital. The handbook said: 'Every possibility of harm because of exposure must be avoided during transportation. While a casualty is being moved, the main object is to keep him warm in every possible way. It is important to equip all transportation facilities for the wounded with an abundant supply of woollen blankets, shelter halves, protective paper wrappings for limbs, and paper vests, socks, and caps. If possible, felt boots should be available for those wounded men who have none of their own. In horse-drawn sleds and ambulances foot-sacks of fur, or woollen blankets, should be available. All sleds and other means of transportation should have a bed of loose straw (in an emergency, fir twigs) or braided straw mats as protection against the cold and jolting.'

(**Opposite, above**) In a village, two horses in tandem can be seen attached to a sled full of supplies. The handbook noted: 'The panje sled generally used in Russia has proved to be the best for the transportation of light loads. Its carrying capacity is small, being commensurate with the draught strength of the panje horse. In midwinter the capacity is frequently not more than 100 pounds.'

(**Opposite, below**) Civilians assisting a unit's advance have halted in the snow with their sleds and horses. A stationary prime mover can be seen. The handbook: 'When adequate equipment is not available for issue, means of transportation can be either confiscated from local inhabitants or constructed by the personnel of the unit. If it is necessary for a unit to construct its own vehicles, particularly sleds, the vehicles of the natives should be used as models. These vehicles have proved their worth for centuries.'

(**Above**) In the chapter 'Winter Bivouacs and Shelter': 'The Eskimo type of igloo (Iglu nach Eskimoart) is a very useful shelter and can be built easily if the snow is deep enough and of the right consistency. It is especially valuable in treeless, uninhabited areas, or when tents are not available. Its construction requires practice and familiarity with snow as a material. The igloo is a domed house made of snow blocks. It offers protection against wind, cold, rifle and machine-gun fire, and shell fragments. It can be used in many ways as a shelter, sentry box, firing position, pillbox, dressing station, refrigerator for foods, and shelter for horses and motor vehicles. It can be occupied throughout the winter … The equipment necessary for constructing igloos consists of the following: 3 whipsaws or fretsaws (length of blades, 16 to 20 inches) for cutting and trimming snow blocks, 4 long-shovels with cross grips for lifting snow blocks, 2 hatchets for cutting ice, 1 hand sled for carrying snow blocks, 1 wooden form (trapezoid shape) for measuring snow blocks, 4 field spades for carving snow blocks, 1 piece of string, 10 feet long, for use as a ground compass and plumb-line during construction … Dry, hard snow, from which snow blocks can be cut quickly, is best suited for building an igloo.'

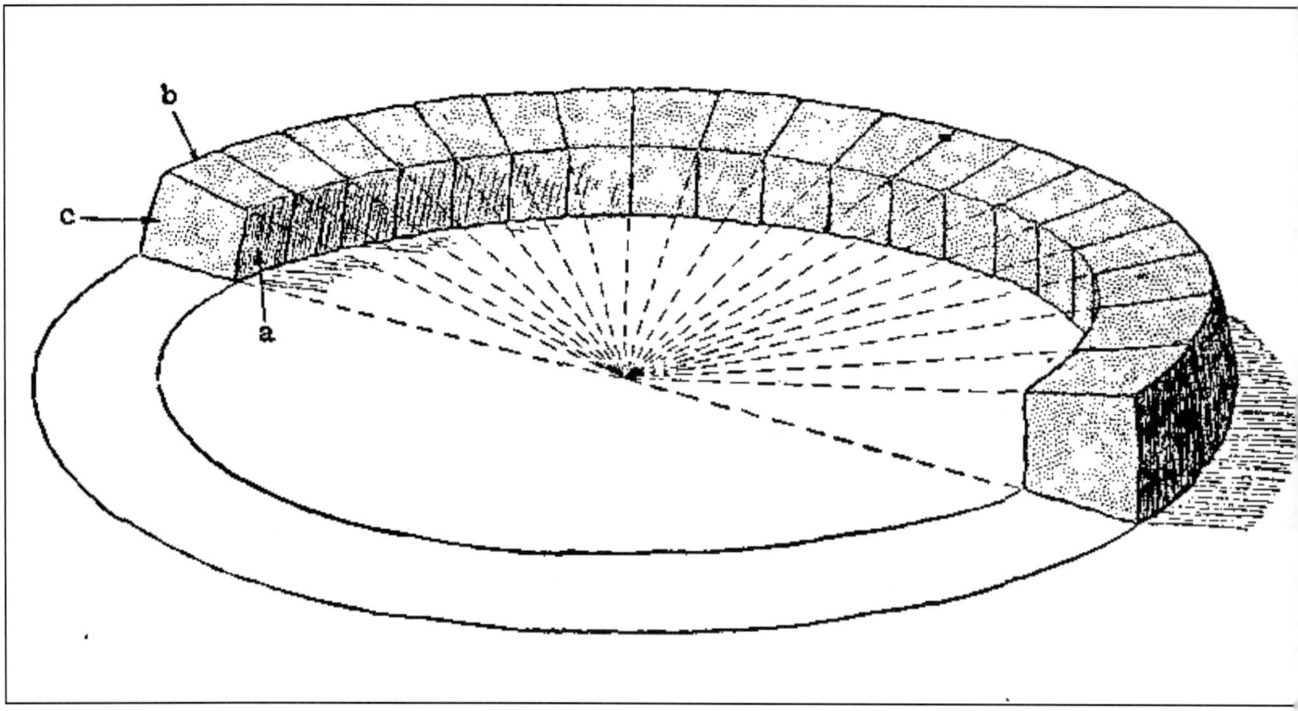
b
c
a

(**Opposite, above**) This diagram shows the layout for the construction of an igloo and the first tier of the shelter: 'The blocks are fitted together within the double lines of the circle marked out in the snow. The surfaces marked 'a,' which are 13 inches long, face inside, and the surfaces marked 'b,' which are 16 inches long, face outside. The thickness of the wall (marked 'c') is 20 inches. A space in the circle, about 24 inches wide, is left open as an entrance on the side away from the enemy. The top surface of the blocks is slanted slightly inward with the saw. The degree of slanting can be determined by using the measuring string and extending it from the centre of the igloo to make a straight line to the outer edge of the blocks. In this way each block is given its final shape and position.'

(**Opposite, below**) Soldiers of the Gebirgsjäger construct an igloo under the supervision of their commanding officer. The soldier on the right is wearing white cotton material wrapped over his Bergmütze and secured at his chin. Opposite him his comrade has the two-piece suit hood worn over the Bergmütze with a pair of snow goggles.

(**Above**) Gebirgsjäger soldiers are seen manhandling a cut block of snow in preparation for constructing an igloo. The handbook stipulates: 'The snow should be at least 12 inches thick. The lower layers under powdery snow may be cut into blocks after the loose snow is removed. Thawing snow can always be used for building an igloo. If the snow is not deep, large snowballs can be made by rolling; then blocks are cut out. The thicker the blocks, the more quickly the building will be finished.'

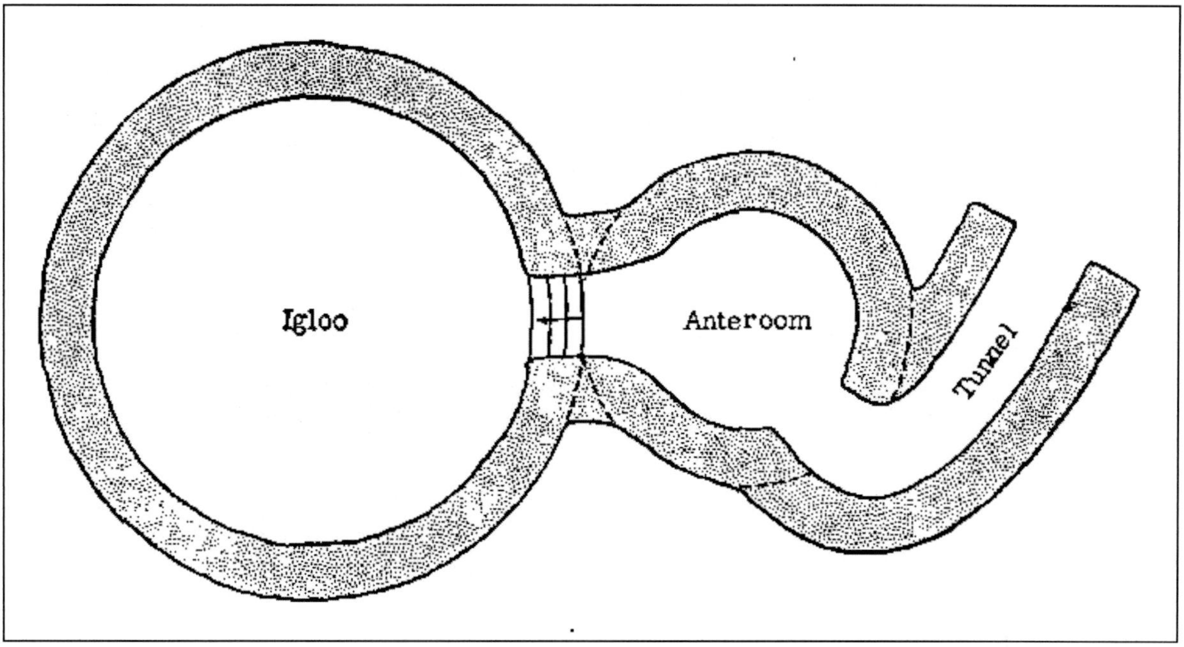

(**Opposite, above**) Gebirgsjäger building an igloo. The entrance of the igloo has been constructed first as outlined in the handbook. 'The blocks of the second tier are placed on the first tier in the same manner, beginning at the entrance gap, and the third tier is also added in the same fashion. To speed up construction, the first three tiers need be cut only roughly. It is important, however, that they form a solid foundation for the upper tiers. Remnants of snow blocks are left inside the igloo during construction, so that the building detail later can stand on the pile to reach the surface of the tier. When the wall is 3 or 4 tiers, or about 50 inches high, the entrance gap is bridged by a long block.'

(**Opposite, below**) In the chapter 'Winter Bivouacs and Shelter' there is a section describing the construction of igloos. This diagram shows the building of the igloo using blocks of cut snow including the entrance to the shelter. Under 'Completing the Dome': 'As the structure grows higher, the diameter of the tier diminishes sharply and the blocks slant more towards the centre of the circle. All blocks at this stage must be cut especially clean and even so that a good fit and adhesion may be obtained. Up to about two-thirds of the height of the igloo construction difficulties increase; then they decrease because the tiers become almost self-supporting as they grow smaller. If newly placed blocks will not adhere, support blocks 4 to 8 inches longer than the others are inserted in at least four places in each tier. Blocks of normal size are joined to them. Thus a vertical adhering surface is provided in addition to the bottom, slanted surface. At this stage of construction two men should hold the blocks in place from the inside with their shoulders and arms, and they should continue this support until the last block is wedged in at the centre of the roof.'

(**Above**) The diagram shows the plans for the 'Tunnel entrance and anteroom of the igloo' under the heading 'Finishing Touches': 'Blocks protruding on the inside are smoothed down. The igloo can be frozen and strengthened by sprinkling it with water up to a height of 4½ feet. The top of the dome, however, should consist only of dry snow, which is best for ventilation and for protection against cold. The outside of the igloo is left rough to provide a holding surface for a cover of snow which will fill in the cracks and further strengthen the structure. The snow is made to serve a double purpose around the lower part of the igloo. Banked to a thickness of 10 feet or more, the snow provides protection against rifle fire and shell fragments. It also camouflages the igloo to make it appear like a snowdrift.'

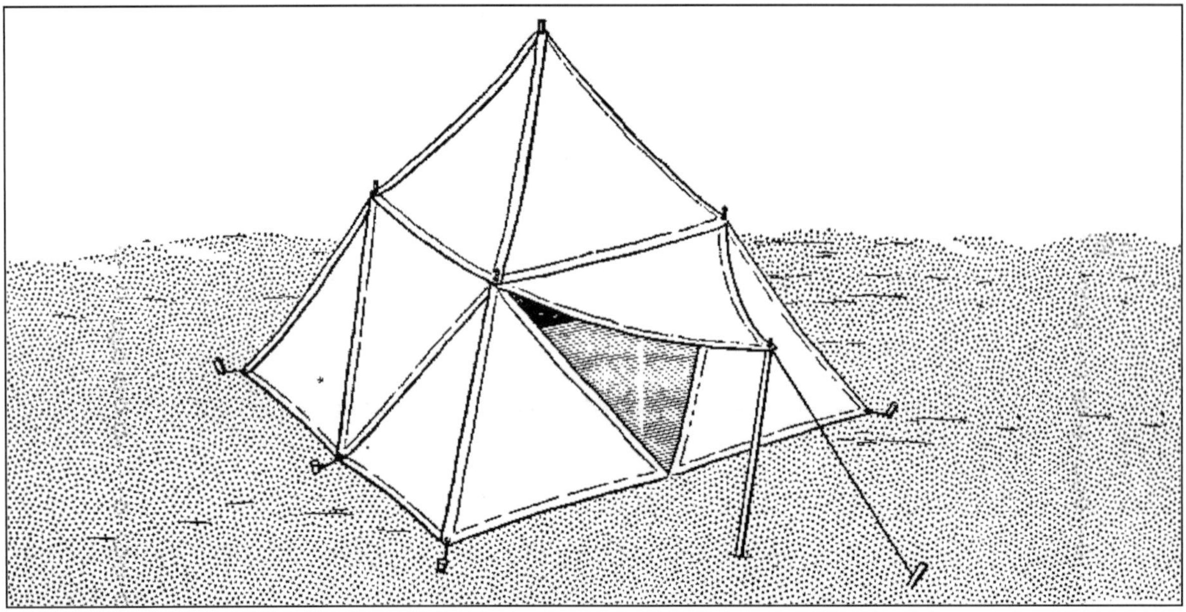

An illustration depicting a sixteen-man tent using Zeltbahn waterproof capes, known as a 'House Tent': 'Tents are the bivouac shelters which can be erected most rapidly for protection against wind and cold. They are easily transported and therefore are especially suited for mobile winter forces. The types of tent shelters discussed here are those made with shelter halves, and circular tents of the Finnish type. The sixteen-man tent made by buttoning together shelter halves, known as a 'house tent' (Hauszelt) is suitable for use as an emergency winter tent because a warming fire or tent stove can be installed in it. It covers an area of about 25 square metres (269 square feet) and is about 9 feet high. It affords shelter for at least 16 men. If the shelter halves are sewed together, the tent may be erected more rapidly and will provide a greater degree of warmth and protection against the wind. Waterproof ground sheets or captured shelter halves should be furnished to men whose regular shelter halves are used in making the 'house tent.'

A drawing showing a circular Finnish type tent (Rundzelt nach Finnischer Art): 'The absence of pegs around the canvas: the canvas folds under to form a floor covering … The Finnish type of circular tent, together with the tent stove, is easy to transport (by man-drawn sled). The tent may be pitched in 15 to 20 minutes. It permits bivouacking in the open at temperatures of -40 degrees F. and below. Thus these tents are especially suitable for mobile winter forces, and it is desirable to issue them to troops.'

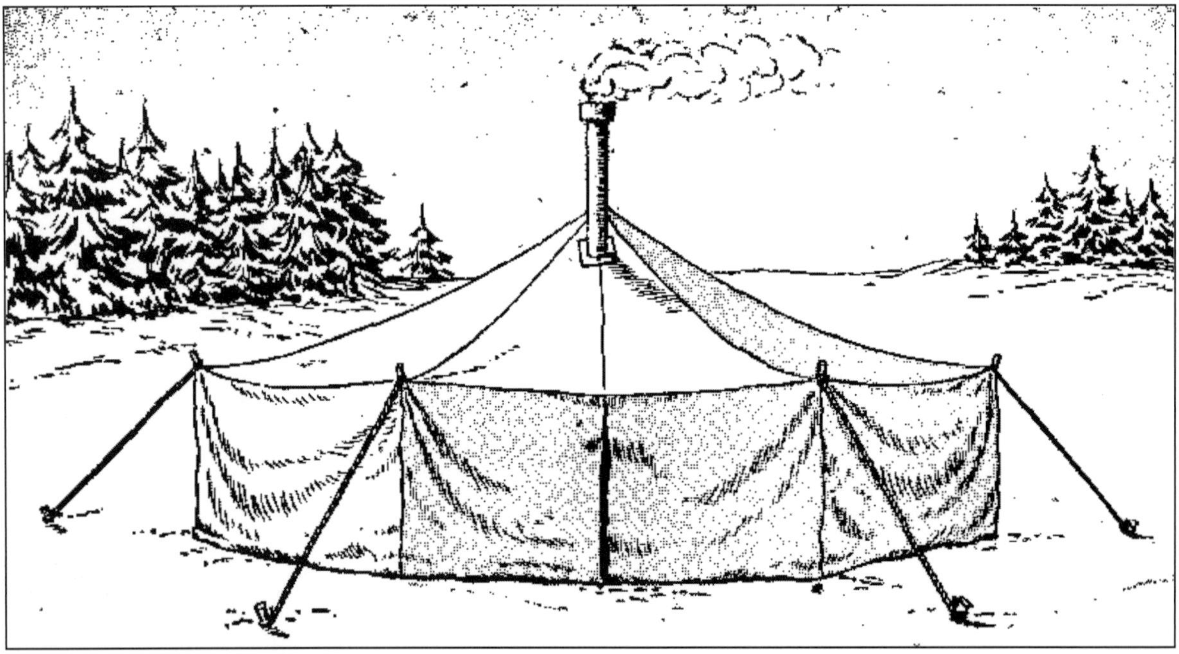

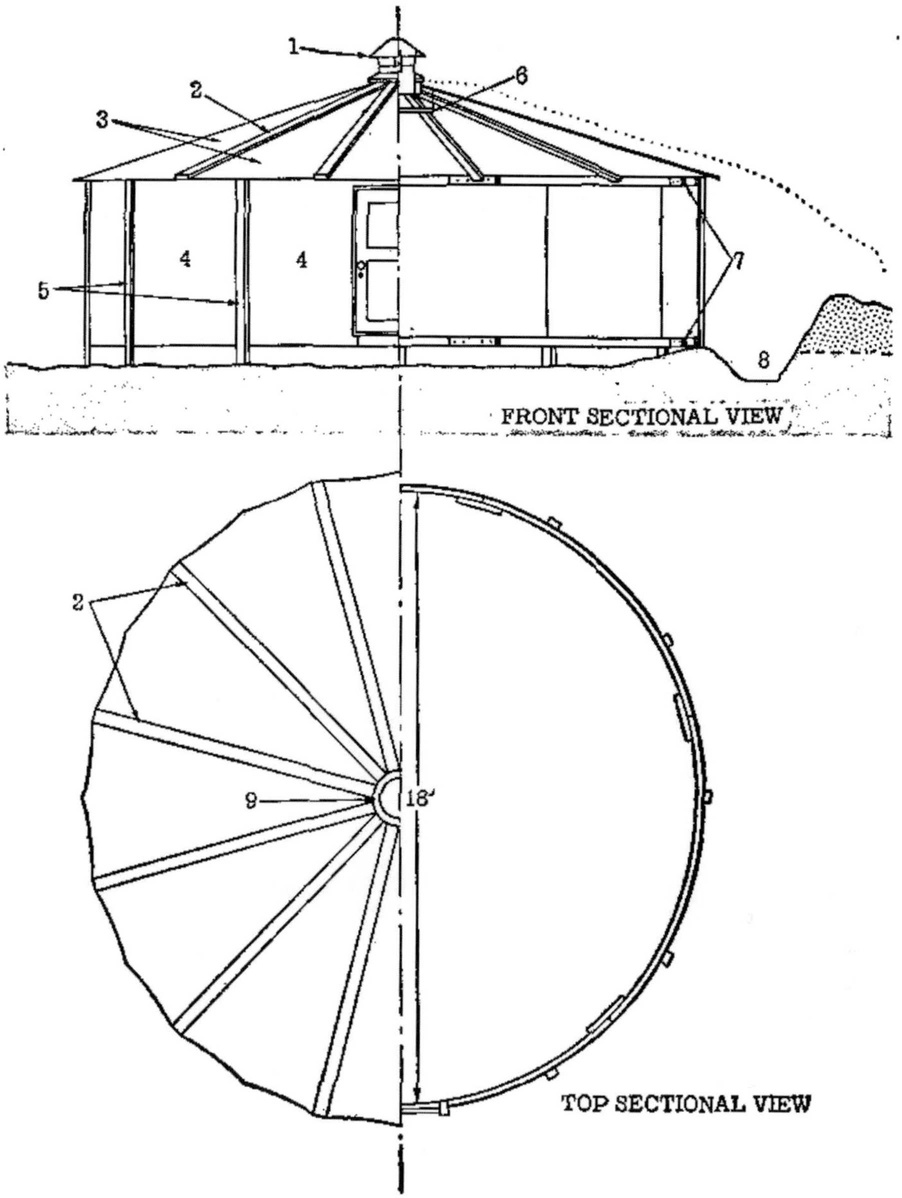

Another form of shelter constructed on the Eastern Front, but regarded more of a permanent structure, was the twenty-man plywood shelter (Sperrholzzelte or Finnenzelte), as seen in this diagram. The handbook described these shelters as 'substitutes for cloth tents. The general-issue prefabricated plywood shelter consists of the following parts: 12 rectangular wall boards, 12 triangular roof boards, 1 support pole, 1 box containing 72 bolts, wing nuts, and washers, 1 mounting ring, 1 ventilation hood in two parts, with 4 rods and 8 wedges.'

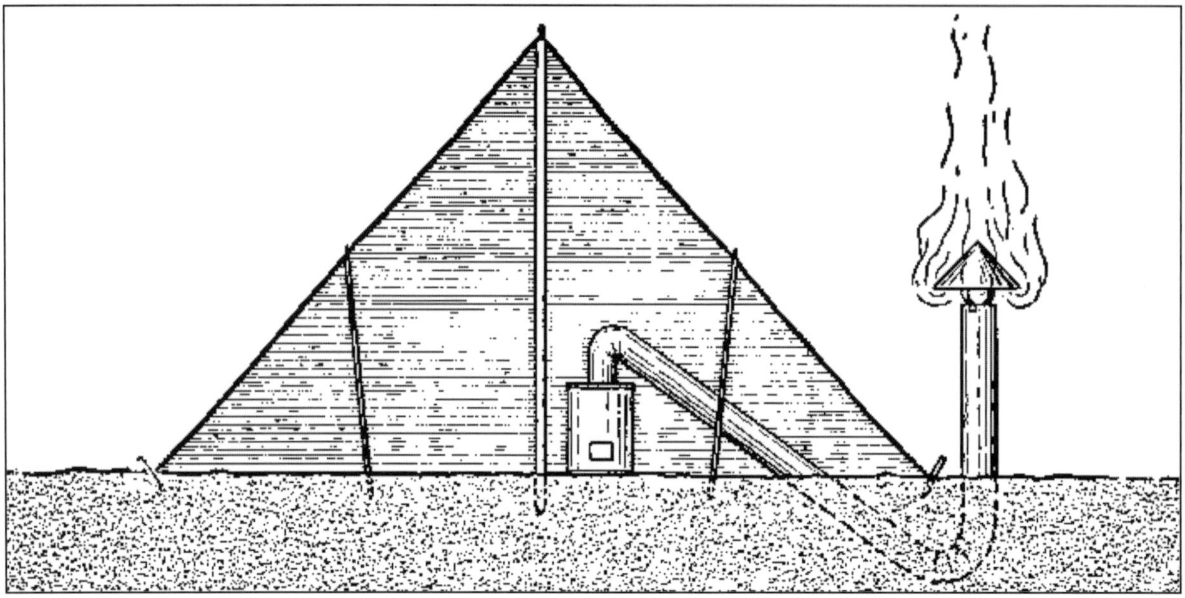

This illustration is titled 'Method of tubing a stove chimney underground': 'If a tent stove is available, the chimney is tubed through the ground into the open to retain as much heat as possible.'

A crude attempt has been made by these SS soldiers to build a branch shelter around a fir tree. The handbook: 'Billets and bivouac shelters, depots, and vehicle parks outside inhabited localities must be established as far as possible in evergreen forests or in dense snow-covered deciduous woods. Trees may be chopped down only if timber is abundant. Clearings which may be visible from the air must be concealed from enemy observation by arching and tying branches together over the open spaces. Care must be taken that the branches are covered with snow … The framework of the branch shelter consists of props and wickerwork made from long shrubbery switches. Fir branches, reeds, or bulrushes are placed upon or woven into the wickerwork in the manner of roof tiling.'

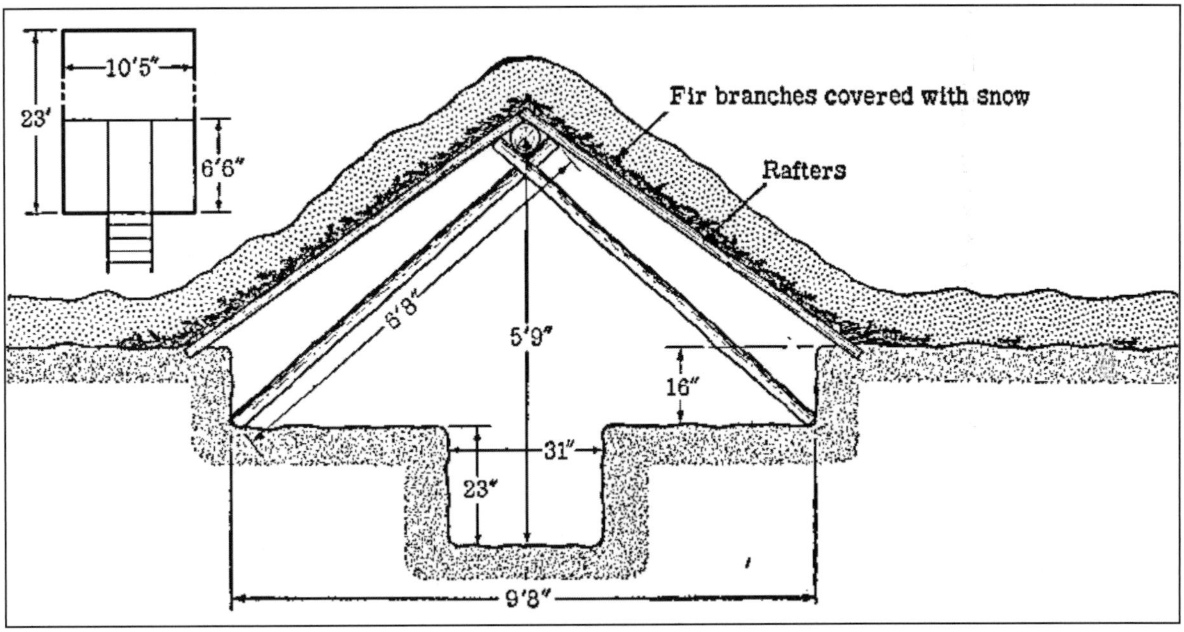

This drawing depicts what the Germans called an 'Earth hut', designed for up to six men. As the diagram outlines, a wooden lean-to framework would be constructed covered with foliage and/or snow.

Here soldiers can be seen in front of what the handbook refers to as 'permanent billets'. The shelter is a wooden-framed structure with earth and foliage covering it. There would be a stove inside the shelter for warmth and heating food and drinks. Because these shelters were of larger construction the work was undertaken by the Construction Service (Heeresbaudienst) with help from the troops. The handbook: 'The units will provide labour details, engineer units, and vehicles. All construction of field-type shelters for smaller units is carried out by the troops themselves.'

Another photograph showing a permanent billet, but of slightly smaller construction, probably built without the help of the Construction Service.

In this diagram from the chapter 'Winter Bivouacs and Shelter': 'The smaller the shelter, the warmer it will be. In snow of lesser depth an open snow hole is dug and covered with snow blocks.'

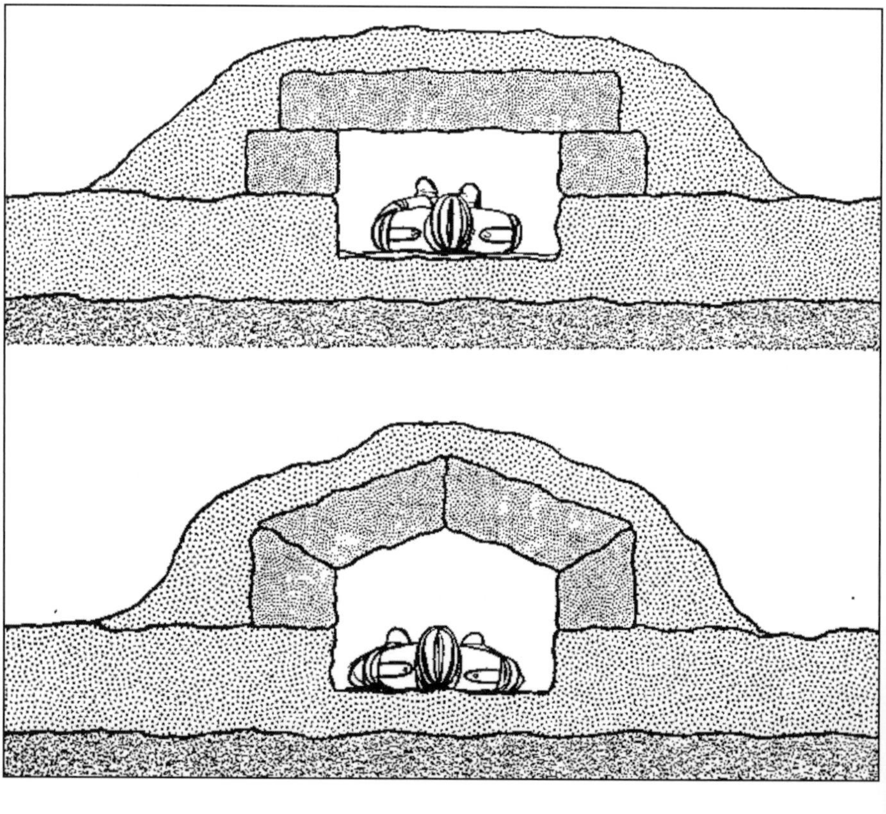

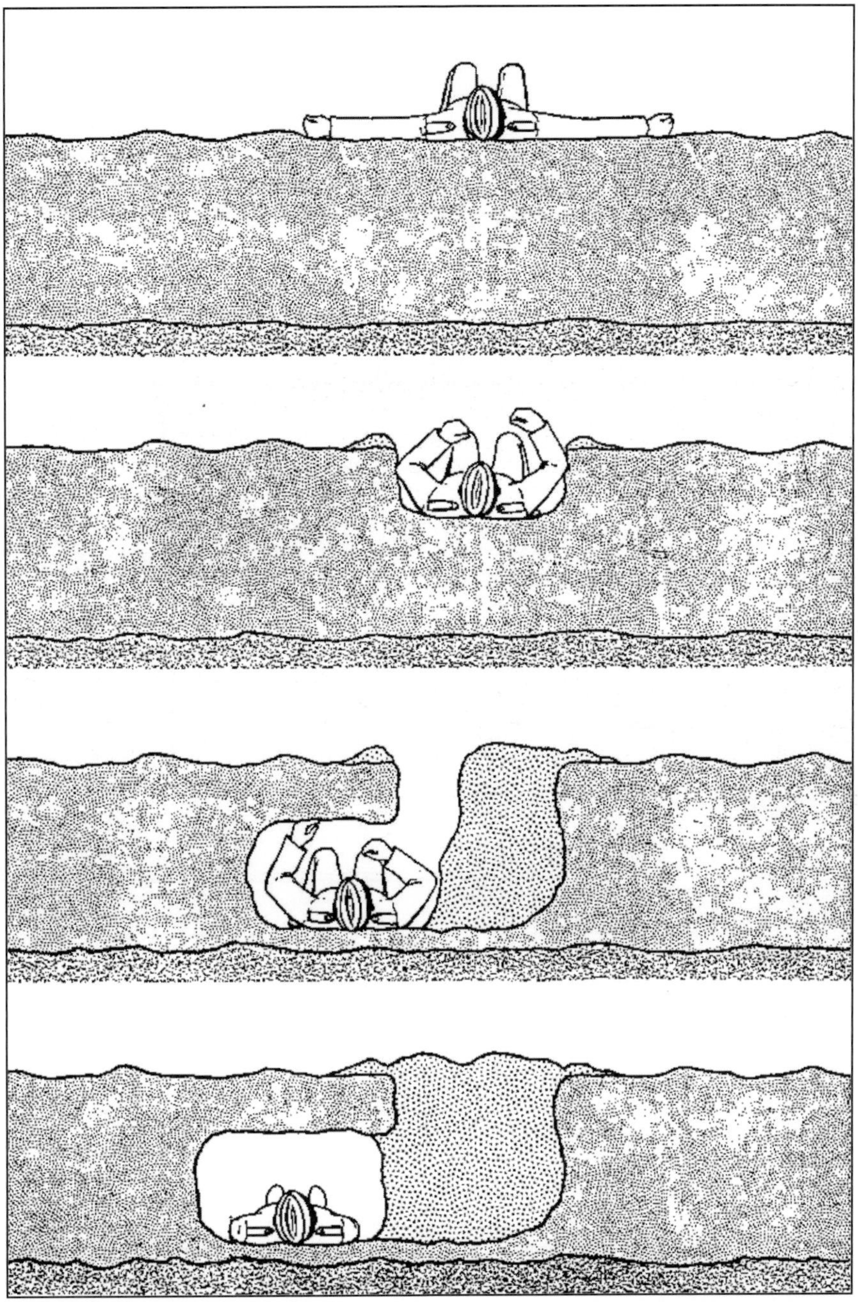

The section 'Winter Bivouacs and Shelter' covers snow shelters, snow caves, snow pits and snow houses. This figure shows how to build a snow hole. The snow hole was an emergency shelter for protection against freezing in a snowstorm, or shelter during a sudden attack. 'Spades, skis, and bayonets may be used for digging it. Even when no tools are available, the soldier can lie on his back on top of snow 20 inches deep and create a hole in a few minutes' – as in this figure. 'He pushes with his feet, digs with his hands, and repeatedly turns over, thereby fashioning a hole the length of his body and the width of his shoulders. When he has reached a 20-inch depth, he digs himself in sideways below the surface, and then fills in the original ditch with the snow he has excavated until only a small opening remains. This opening may be entirely closed, depending upon the enemy situation and the temperature.'

This diagram shows the building of a 'snow pit'. It informs the soldier: 'The snow pit is dug vertically into the snow in the same fashion as the snow hole, but it is larger and rectangular. Skis, sticks, poles, branches, shelter halves, and snow are used as roofing. The pit affords shelter for several men in a prone position. It is advisable to slope the roof down towards the foot end.'

The diagram describes the construction of a 'snow house with walls of ice blocks'. It tells the soldier, 'The size and the roof of snow houses are similar to those of snow pits. The side walls, however, consist of snow blocks and may be built, even in case of a light snow, up to the height of a man. Snow piled on the outside seals the cracks and camouflages the building.'

In the chapter 'Construction of Winter Positions': 'If it is impossible to dig in because of frozen ground, deep snow, or lack of time, cover above ground level must be provided by stacking sandbags to form walls which may be hardened by pouring water over them. Sandbags of cloth soak up water more readily than paper bags. The outside of the walls must be plastered with snow. Trampling increases the hardness of the snow. On top of the trampled snow, loose clean snow must be scattered for camouflage. The floor of rifle pits must be padded with a layer of foliage or fir branches. Such positions afford practical cover and are not easily detected by the enemy.'

The building of a position during winter operations using the surrounding terrain and wooden logs.

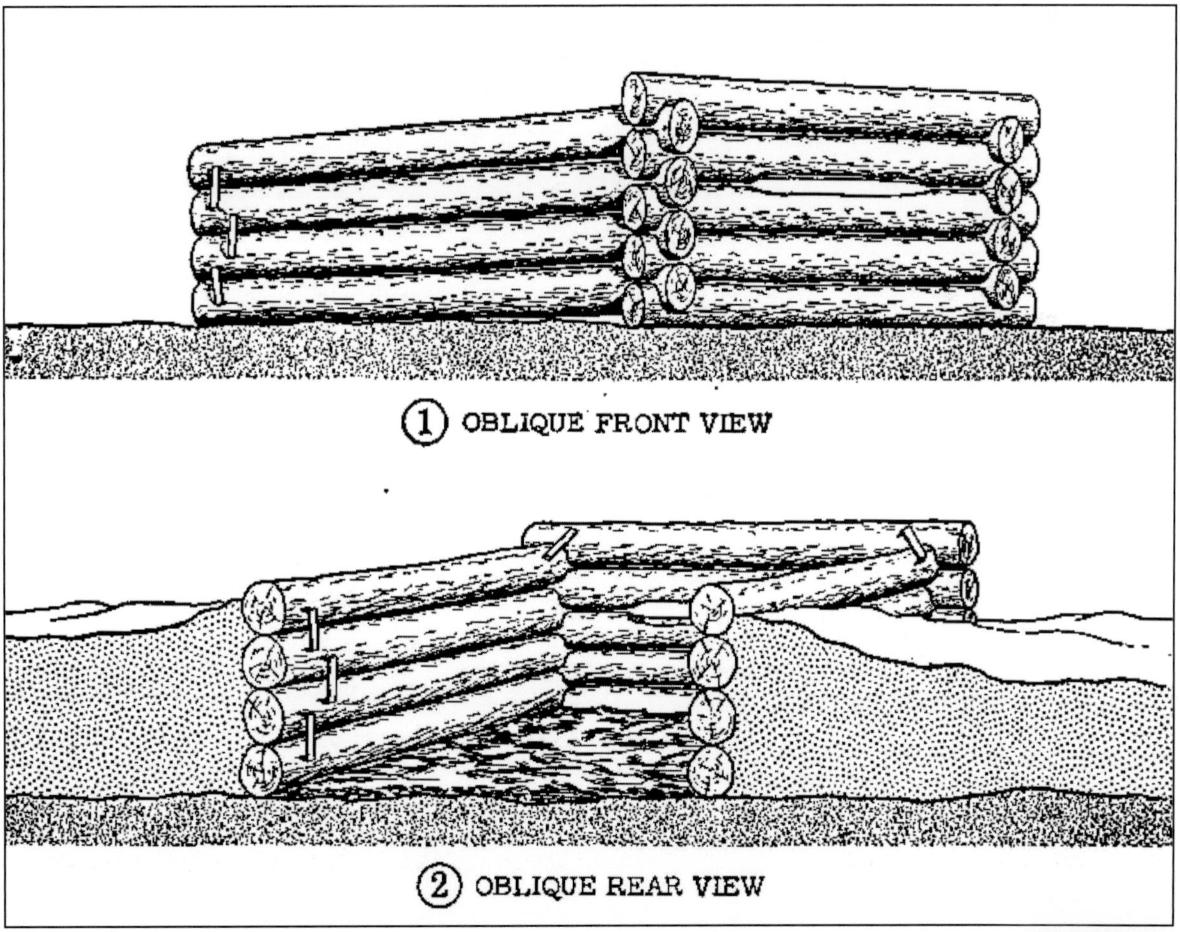

(**Above**) This photograph shows a shelter erected against a hillside as instructed by the handbook. There were principles governing the construction of the various shelters, depending on the type of shelter and the 'period of occupancy'. The shorter the time of occupancy, the more primitive billets would be. In the case of extended use, 'adequate sanitary conditions and comfort must be assured … The type of billets which will be constructed depends on the material available. In densely wooded areas log houses will be constructed; in regions poor in timber, turf houses; in mountainous terrain, stone huts; in the vicinity of sawmills or lumber yards, framework construction; near brickyards, brick construction.'

(**Opposite, above**) This drawing depicts a horse shelter with windbreaks and shelters made of snow and snow blocks.

(**Opposite, below**) In the chapter 'Construction of Winter Positions': 'When the ground is frozen too hard for the digging of trenches, snow walls may be used for cover instead. These walls afford protection against rifle bullets and shell splinters from small-calibre guns as follows: Newly fallen snow … At least 13 feet, Firmly frozen snow … At least 8 to 10 feet, Packed snow … At least 6½ feet, Ice … At least 39 inches. Such walls may be used for constructing covered snow trenches. The inner walls should be lined, the lining being nailed to simple triangular racks. The trench may be deepened later. It is then covered with snow as heavily as possible. A communication trench may also be built in this way and it would offer good concealment and protection from shell splinters. The roofing prevents the trench from filling up with drifting snow.'

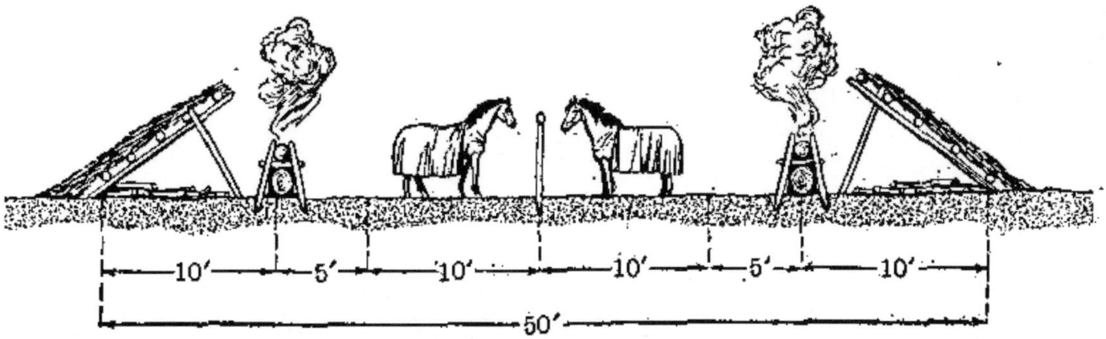

① Horse sheltered by windbreaks

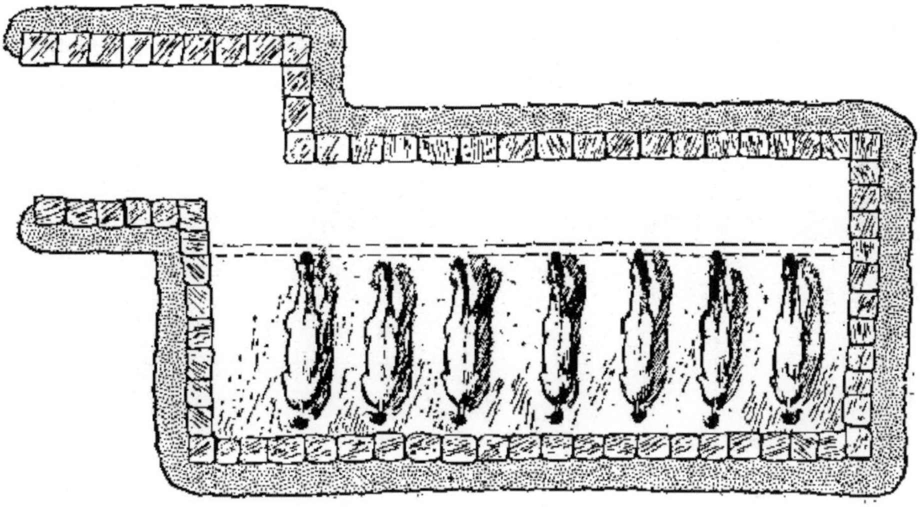

② Shelter made with snow and snow blocks

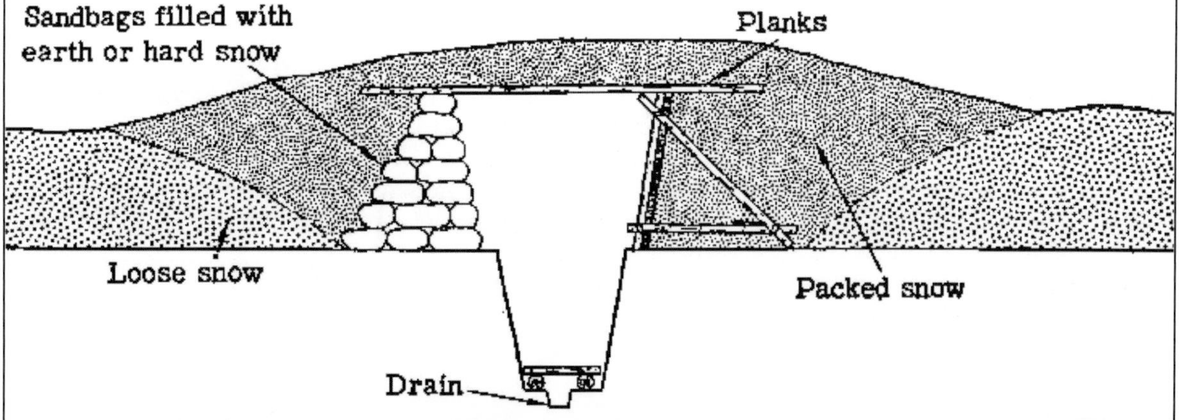

This cross-section drawing shows a 'Vaulted Cave Dugout' system: 'In deep snow, simple caves and dugouts may be dug quickly. They afford protection against inclement weather and small shell splinters and have the advantage of complete camouflage. Such shelters are most substantial when they are vaulted and lined with boards, or they should be reinforced with wooden frames. In long caves, tubes or wooden boxes must be inserted in the ceiling at intervals to provide lighting and ventilation.'

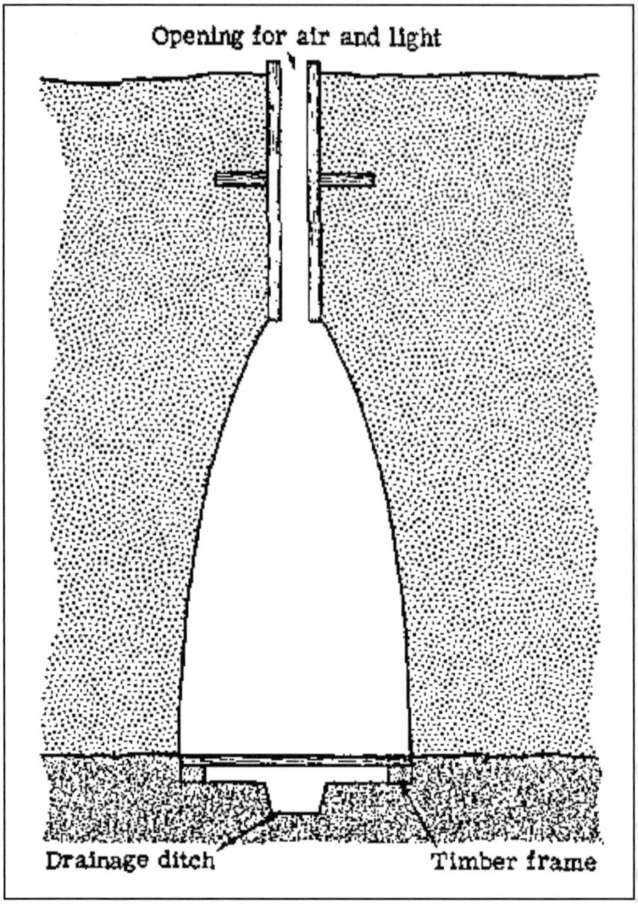

In the chapter 'Camouflage, Concealment and Identification', this drawing depicts camouflaging a trench system using wood frames from surrounding trees: 'Trenches must be camouflaged by covering them as thoroughly as possible within the available time. Mats and wooden frames woven with wire or willow branches may serve as a covering. They must be 5 or 6 feet wide, and long enough to span the trench. The frames are covered with brushwood and weatherproofed with straw or paper which has been previously wet and frozen. After the trench has been covered, camouflage is completed by adding a thin layer of snow. A cover of this type may be raised on supports on the side facing the enemy so that observation and firing are possible.'

Infantry rest in a trench dug out of the snow during operations in central Russia. The handbook stipulated that trench systems 'must be camouflaged by covering them as thoroughly as possible within the available time.'

Infantry digging a trench in a forest area. The handbook: 'An infantryman digging a foxhole in open, snow-covered country offers a good target if the pile of excavated snow is too high, or if earth is mingled with the snow. Excavated earth must be integrated into surrounding ground features and covered with snow. When observing or firing from a parapet, the snow must be scooped out to keep the soldier's silhouette low and to avoid showing his head in relief.'

What appears to be a forward observation post and a soldier surveys the snowy terrain ahead using a pair of binoculars from the entrance of his snow cave. The handbook says: 'Where the situation permitted and the depth and consistency of the snow was suitable, types of snow shelters that proved effective were the snow hole, the snow cave, the snow pit, the snow house, and the Eskimo-type igloo.'

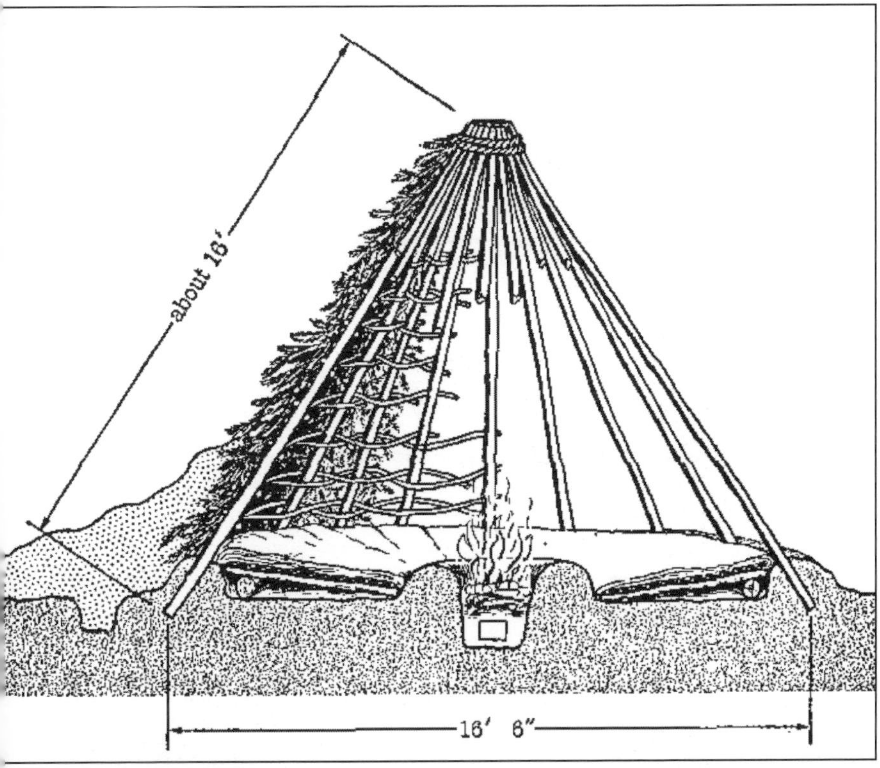

In the section 'Lean-tos and other improvised shelters', this drawing shows a typical lean-to shelter constructed from logs and branches in a forest area under a fir tree: 'The denser the walls are woven and the tighter they are plastered with earth and snow, the warmer the huts will be. With heat furnished by log-fires or stoves, they may be suitable even for overnight stops in winter. For just a few men the simplest structure is the circular shelter, built around trees, or the circular hut made of branches.'

Waffen-SS troops are seen in a shallow trench system dug inside a forest. There appears to be a crude shelter erected against a fir tree, using a waterproof Zeltbahn cape for additional protection. This position was known in the handbook as 'primitive billet for shorter occupancy'.

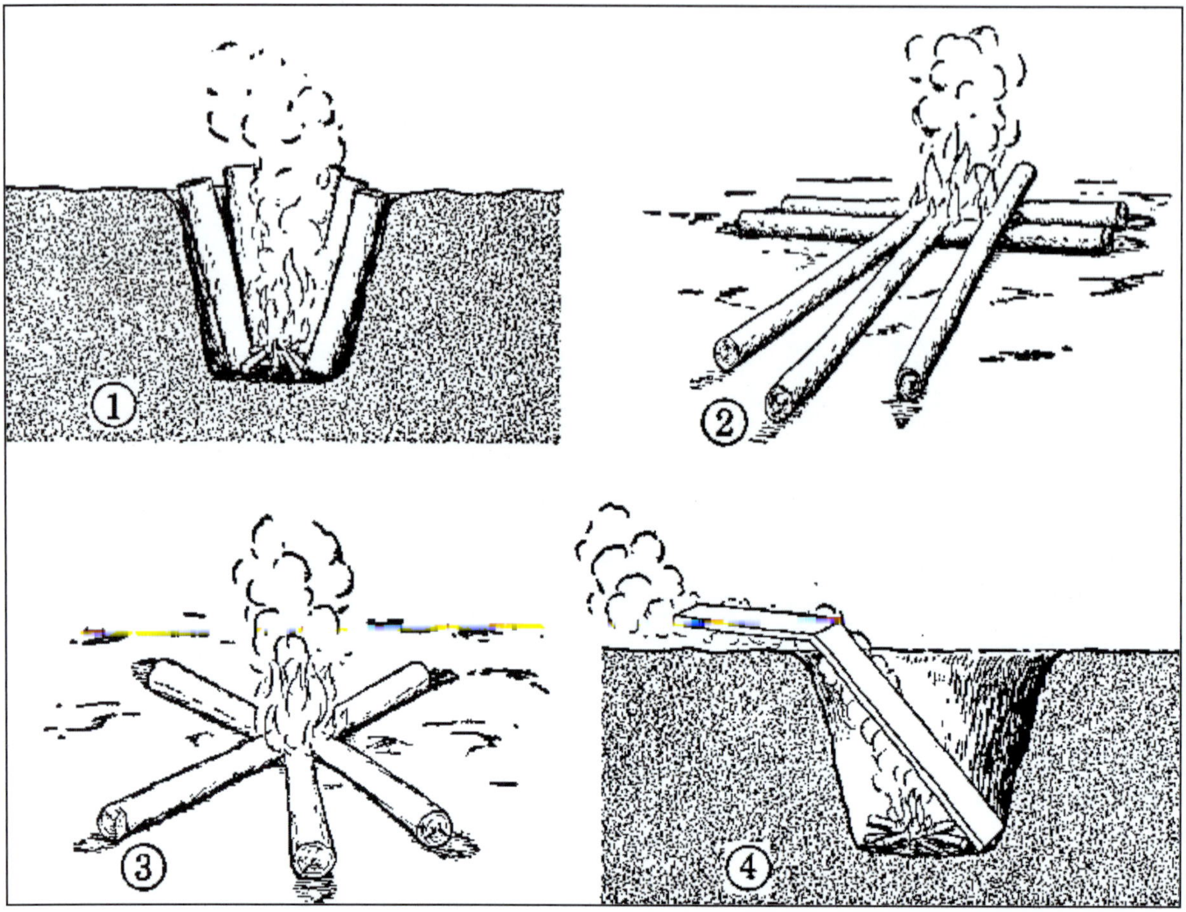

(**Above**) In the chapter 'Heating Facilities' this picture shows (1) pit fire; (2) hunter's fire; (3) star-shaped fire; (4) 'invisible fire.' The pit fire 'gives warmth and also furnishes charcoal. Stand the wood in the pit; not much is needed.' The hunter's fire: 'Place logs in a fan formation on top of two other logs. Light the fire where the logs cross each other, and keep pushing the logs into the fire as the ends burn away. This fire burns slowly and warms well.' The star-shaped fire: 'Shove the logs forward as they burn.' The invisible fire 'is made in a deep pit. Then place a piece of bark or wood over the fire with one end bent and projecting flat over the edge of the pit. The smoke will be led off horizontally and dissipated without betraying the fire.'

(**Opposite, above**) These two drawings describe the various methods of installing heating for emplacements and caves and in trench position using a stove. For the emplacement and caves the handbook describes the best way of using the heating facility: 'Hot stones contained in a grate or a box filled with paper or straw are useful for heating small shelters, such as sentry boxes. Similar expedients are especially suitable for warming the wounded while they are being evacuated; in addition to hot stones, warming bottles filled with hot water or hot sand, paper, cloth and fur wrappings, and blankets may be used.' In a trench it describes using an insulated stove: 'Various types of field stoves are being issued, and can be insulated with stones to retain the heat. Instructions for their use should be followed precisely. In the front lines only charcoal should be used (fire without smoke).' The section also covered brick stoves with ovens, making charcoal, and covered the dangers of carbon-monoxide poisoning.

(**Opposite, below**) The section 'Permanent Billets' covers construction of various shelters, including 'Heated shelter for motor vehicles', as in this drawing.

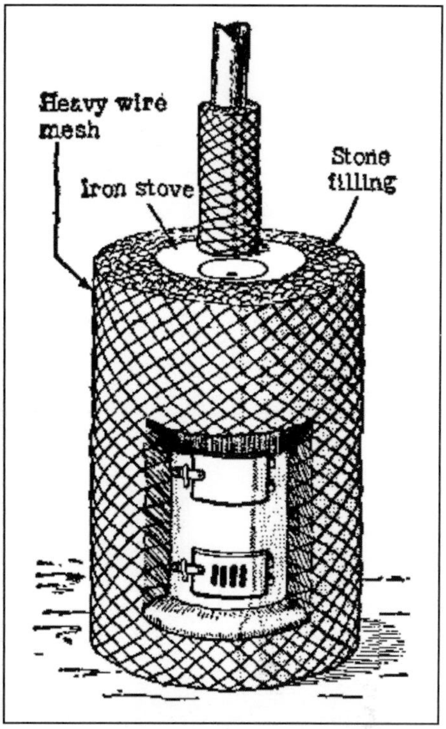

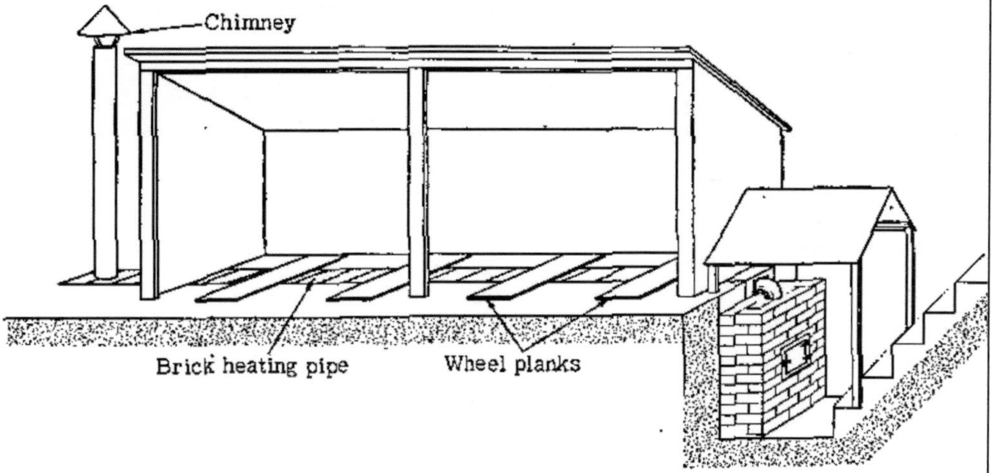

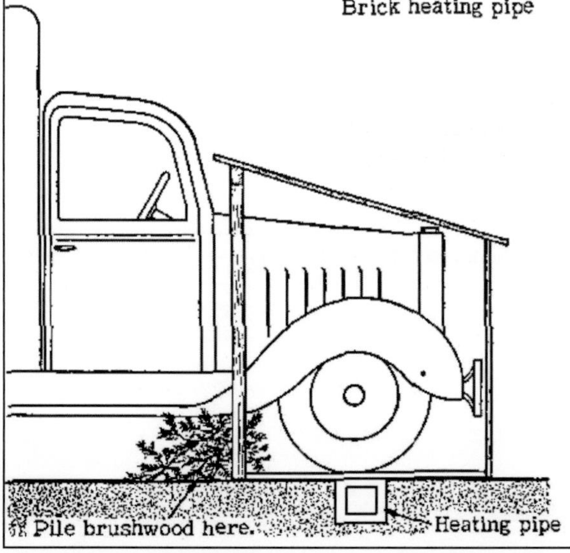

Make the heating pipes out of bricks. Iron pipes might be hazardous if gasoline drips on them. Cement pipes crack easily. If shelter is available for the motor only, pack brushwood under the driver's seat to keep the heat from escaping.

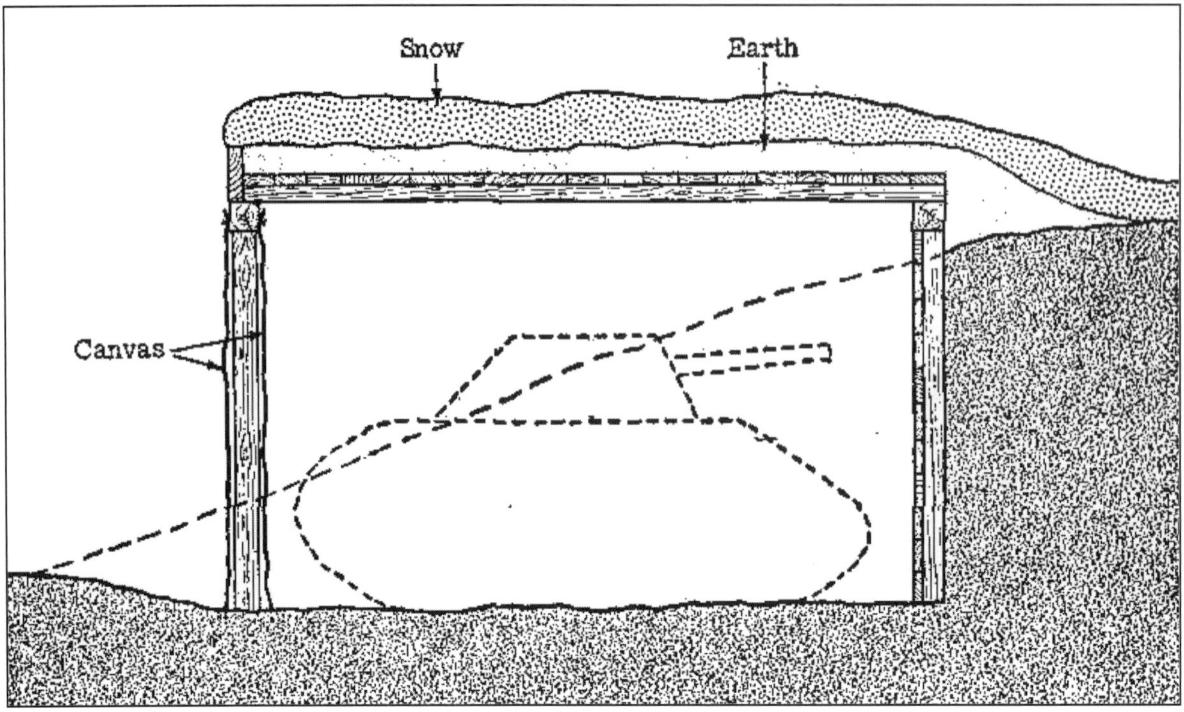

This diagram shows a 'Tank shelter built against a slope'. A wooden frame structure has been built around the vehicle and snow and earth placed on the roof. Canvas sheeting has been used for the entrance and exit point of the shelter.

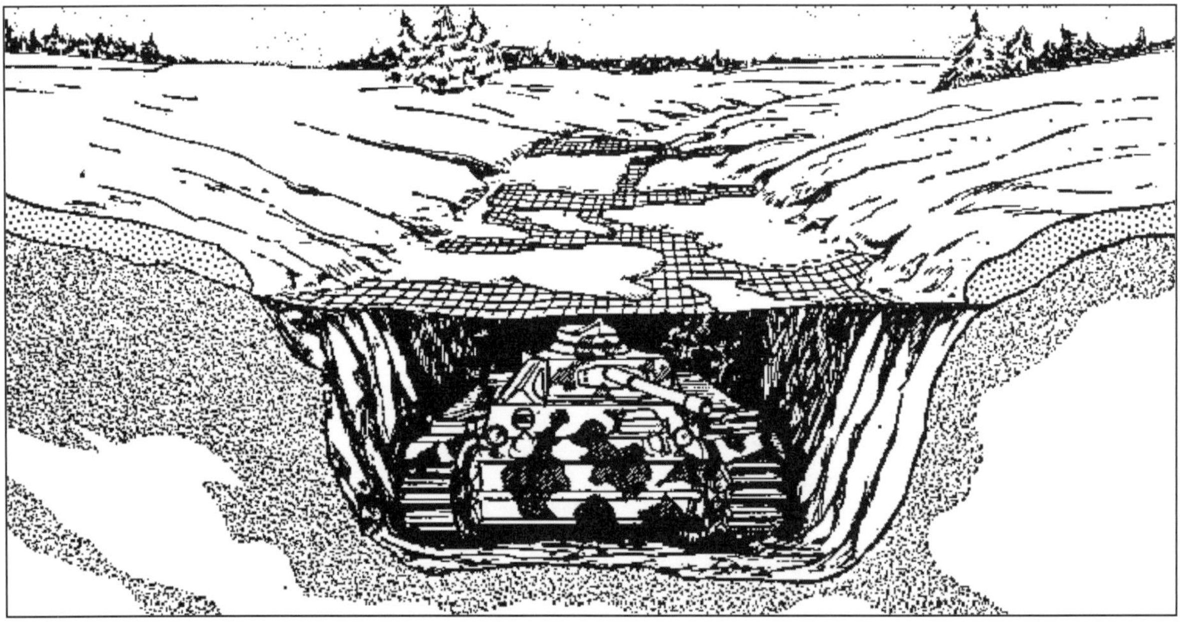

This drawing shows a tank concealed in a gully and hidden under camouflage netting and foliage.

Ways to camouflage a tank in the field using a snow-covered canvas.

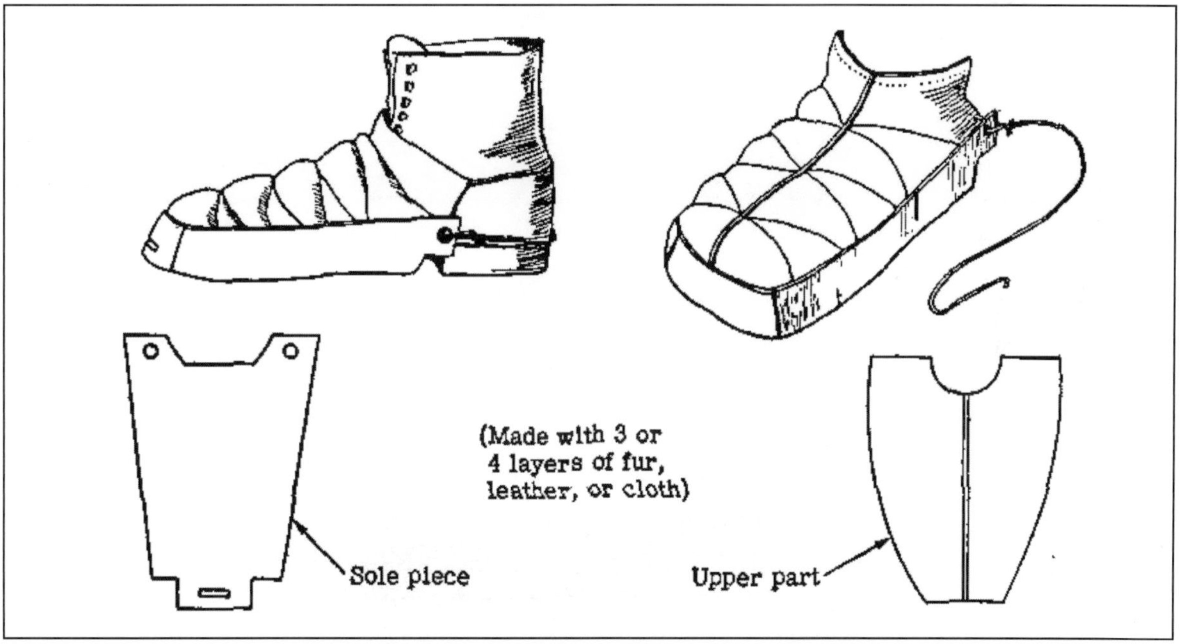

In the chapter 'Protection against cold, snow and thaw', rations, maintenance of health, care of weapons, equipment and ammunition, care of motor vehicles, care of horses, heating facilities, and most of all clothing, are covered. This diagram shows improvising by additional insulation of shoes and boots: 'An especially effective measure for protecting the feet is to wear paper between two pairs of socks, and another layer of paper or foot cloths over the top pair of socks. All wrinkles must be smoothed out. If ski boots are worn, a piece of cloth should be sewed over the heels of the socks to prevent wear at that point. Boot leather can be kept from freezing by covering the shoes or boots with the foot of a sock or a casing made of fur or similar material.'

'The feet are especially susceptible to frostbite. Socks should be changed frequently. A proved measure for preventing frostbite of the feet is to use inner soles of straw, cloth, or paper; the straw should be cut to the right size and arranged carefully; if newspaper is used, it should be wrapped carefully around the foot to avoid wrinkles. Foot cloths (also paper 'foot cloths') are warmer than socks.'

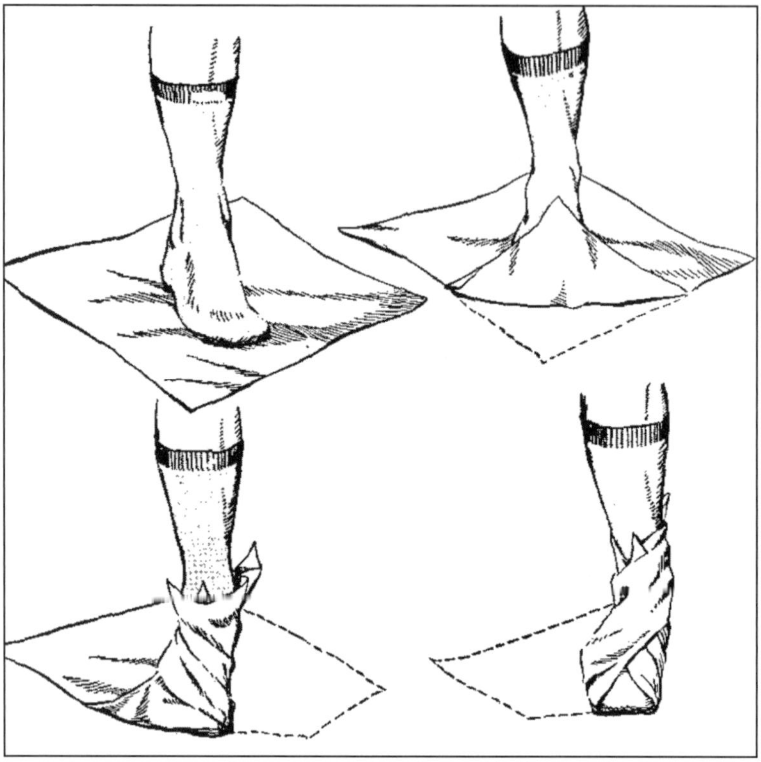

A Waffen-SS radio operator can be seen operating a lightweight radio. These soldiers are probably at a forward observation post, from where they can send details of enemy movements back to divisional headquarters.

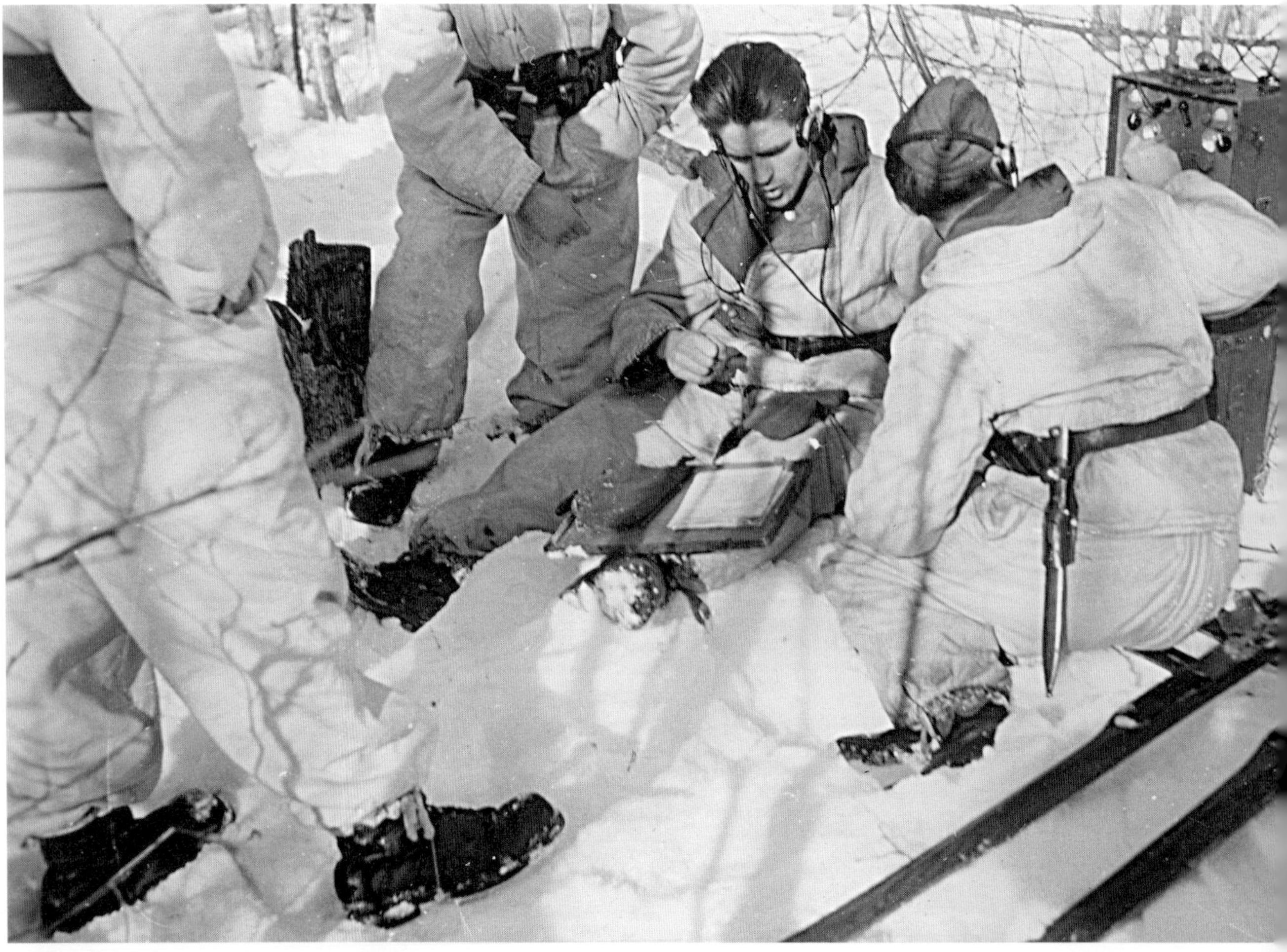

Infantry clad in their winter whites march across the snow with a sled full of supplies being pulled by animals. The soldier is wearing a whitewashed steel helmet and carries an ammunition box. The handbook noted that for emergency precautions against the cold, 'put felt lining inside the steel helmet – preferably the crown of an old felt hat. If nothing else is available, use a handkerchief or crumpled newspaper. The strap should be worn loose so that circulation of the blood will not be impaired.'

(**Above**) Infantry marching across the snow. The handbook noted: 'On the march and in combat the following practices should be observed. Use breaks in the march and rest periods to exchange unserviceable articles of clothing and to make minor repairs. Garments left behind by wounded men should be collected and turned in without exception. In snowstorms wear the fur coat inside out and wrap a shelter half around it if it does not conflict with camouflage requirements. Even during a temporary halt the troops should take time out to mend and clean their clothes. Particular attention should be devoted to drying wet clothes and, above all, footgear. Do not let boots or shoes dry near a fire or burning stove, because, in addition to the danger that they may burn, they may become hard and brittle. Wet footgear should be stuffed with straw or paper. Snow is an enemy of leather, and the best protection is to keep the leather soft. Care of the footgear is especially important in preparing for a march. The uppers should be greased daily, preferably when damp. Leather which has been greased too much, however, chills the feet and permits water to seep through. This treatment should not be applied just before marches, but well in advance.'

(**Opposite, above**) An infantryman, more than likely at a forward observation post, is wearing his two-piece snow-suit with an identification band on his left arm. The handbook noted: 'In extremely cold weather the steel helmet should be worn over the field cap and the knitted woollen cap. The ears must not come in contact with the metal of the helmet.'

(**Opposite, below**) The crew of a whitewashed 8.8cm FlaK preparing for a mission against a ground target. They are all wearing two-piece snow suits. Note the Sd.Ah 202 limber next to the gun position. The limber was placed close to the weapon so it could be limbered up and moved to another position quickly.

(**Opposite, above**) Here a soldier, a Gebirgsjäger, in southern Russia, wears one of a variety of animal-skin greatcoats, known as Watchmantel (guard overcoat) or Steppenmantel (Steppe overcoat) that were supplied to troops in the second winter.

(**Opposite, below**) A soldier wearing a two-piece snow camouflage suit walks through a captured Russian town. He is wearing a coloured armband on his left arm, which enabled German troops to distinguish between friend and foe. In the section of the handbook 'Means of Identification' it describes how difficult it was to differentiate between friend and foe in winter conditions, even at short distances. 'Therefore,' it read, 'the use of certain distinguishing marks is necessary, and the troops must be advised in orders of their meaning. For individual identification, brassards in two colours (black and red), about 3 inches wide, are worn. They can be buttoned either on the right or left sleeve. To avoid imitation by the enemy, they can be changed periodically, just like passwords. Eight different ways of wearing the brassards are possible, as follows: (a) Black brassard on left upper arm, (b) Black brassard on right upper arm, (c) Black brassard on both upper arms, (d) Red brassard on left upper arm, (e) Red brassard on right upper arm, (f) Red brassard on both upper arms, (g) Black brassard on left upper arm and red brassard on right upper arm, (h) Black brassard on right upper arm and red brassard on left upper arm.'

(**Above**) Regular, SS-Polizei and Gebirgsjäger troops during operations in Army Group North. The soldiers are wearing the standard greatcoat, winter whites and a variety of headgear and have hitched a lift aboard a whitewashed Pz.Kpfw.III.

Two soldiers wearing animal-skin greatcoats. These coats, varying greatly in size and quality, were designed to be worn in extreme cold climates. They were normally worn by officers, but soldiers were also seen wearing them, especially on guard duty. Note the soldier on the right, who appears to be wearing a pair of aviator goggles to protect his eyes from the arctic wind and blizzards.

Chapter Three

The Third Winter 1943/44

The first weeks of 1943 saw the German forces of Army Group South trying to hold their forces together against overwhelming Soviet superiority. Troops situated along the Don were hard pressed to hold their positions especially after the Soviet capture of Bataysk, a suburb of Rostov on the southern bank of the river. In early February further problems arose at Rostov and Voroshilovograd.

In January Hitler gave von Manstein free rein to do whatever he wanted. Using reinforcements from France, and from Army Groups North and Centre, he began a series of counterstrokes against Russian positions. After weeks of severe fighting Kharkov and Kursk were taken. But as problems beset the German forces in the snow, Soviet high command decided to launch a huge counter-attack, hoping to drive the Germans out of the Ukraine forever. Soviet forces simultaneously advanced west from the Donets bend around Isyum forcing German divisions across the icy plains westward. As the Russians pushed further west, Kharkov was recaptured on 16 February. Rostov was abandoned on 18th, and in March Red Army units captured Kursk and Belgorod. They then attacked Army Group Centre in the salient at Orel before breaking out towards Bryansk.

Despite the German retreat, the Soviet attack was proving more difficult than they first envisaged. The German divisions in the south had survived their battering in surprisingly good shape, mainly because the German soldier was flexible and had quickly adapted to his winter surroundings. Unlike 1941/2, when units had become bogged down in seas of mud, commanders now brought forward supplies in good time. Some Panzer units had enough strength and supplies to launch counterattacks, and elite Waffen-SS units fought their way back to Kharkov, where the Germans retook the city again.

The Germans then began planning an ambitious offensive in the Kursk sector. What followed in early July 1943 would be the failed battle of Kursk.

Within three months of the defeat at Kursk, Army Groups Centre and South had been pushed back an average distance of 150 miles on a 650-mile front. The Soviets lost no time in regaining as much territory as possible.

When the winter arrived in early November 1943, despair and gloom gripped the German front lines. The summer and autumn battles had sapped their energy, and now they were faced with another hard winter. To many of the soldiers there was a dull conviction that the war was lost, and yet there was still no end in sight. In the latter half of 1943 the equipment situation continued to deteriorate for the Germans, in contrast to the enormous volume of armaments being produced by the Russians.

Unlike 1941 and 1942, the Germans no longer had the initiative. Slowly they were beaten back across the bleak and hostile landscape, always outnumbered, constantly low on fuel, ammunition and other supplies. To make matters worse, Ukrainian nationalist partisans, Polish underground groups and communist partisans began raiding German outposts, barracks, police stations, rail depots, supply dumps, and ambushing convoys and trains, as snipers picked off exposed soldiers one by one. All this, and continuous pressure from Hitler to defend every yard of land with their blood, made life more grim than ever for the German soldier.

Moving along a trench system during winter operations these soldiers are wearing reversible winter uniform, white side out. Beneath their whitewashed helmet they wore the black woollen toque. The toque was designed to help contain as much body heat as possible and to prevent discomfort from the arctic temperatures while wearing the standard issue steel helmet. Troops often complained that the helmets were like 'freezer boxes' during the winter.

An MG34 machine gunner smiles as he becomes submerged waist deep in snow during a march in early winter 1943. He wears the reversible winter uniform white side out.

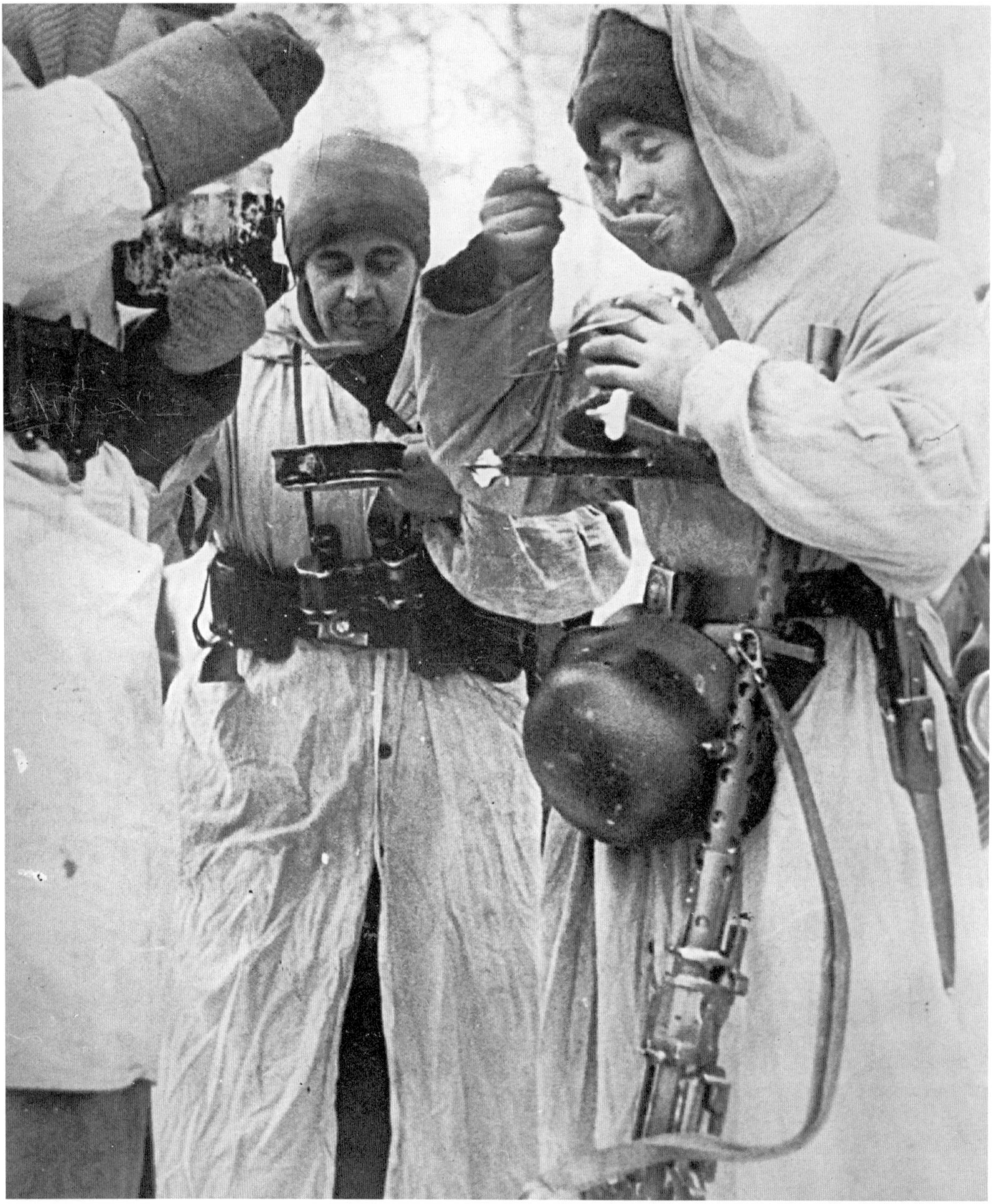

An MG34 crew tuck into their rations using their mess tins. By this time the German soldier had learnt to adapt to the harsh arctic conditions of the Soviet Union. The Russian soldier was accustomed to cold temperatures, which they withstood on far smaller rations than many in the West would have believed possible. Faced with such a foe, the German soldier had to adapt quickly or die.

An MG34 position using logs from the forest to protect themselves from enemy fire. Both soldiers wear the winter reversibles, but note how dirty the suits have become.

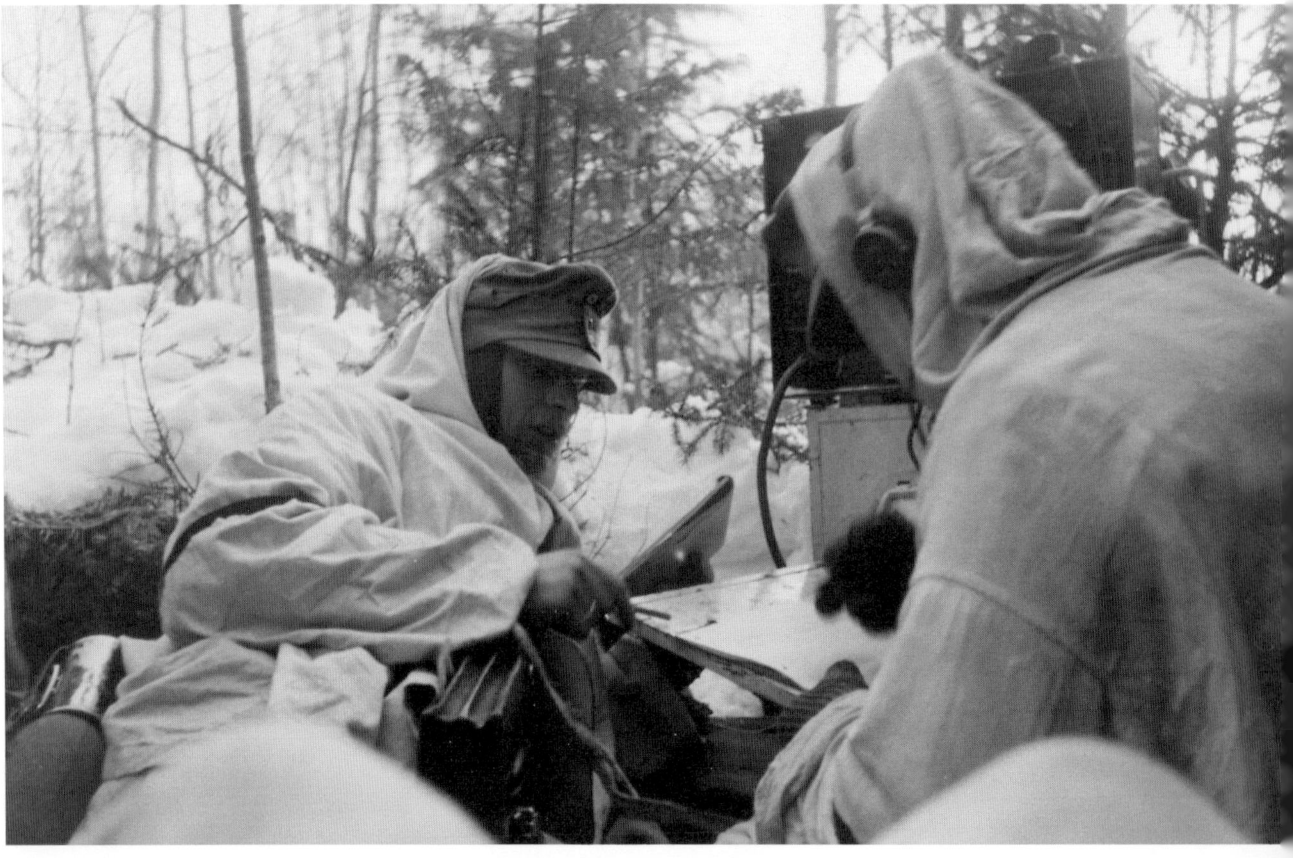

(**Opposite, above**) A Gebirgsjäger soldier on patrol is seen with a dog pulling a sled across the snow. The mountain trooper wears a two-piece snowsuit and is armed with a Kar 98k bolt-action rifle which has received an application of whitewash.

(**Opposite, below**) At a forward observation post, radio operators of the Gebirgsjäger are seen using a lightweight radio while looking at a map.

(**Above**) Battle-worn soldiers wearing the two-piece snow suit can be seen on the march supported by a whitewashed Sturmgeschütz III assault gun.

(**Opposite, above**) During the opening phase of the Battle of Kharkov in late February 1943. The MG34 machine gun is mounted on the Lafette 34 tripod mount which weighed 20.5kg. The optimum operating crew of an MG34 for sustained fire operation was six men. The gunner was known as the No. 1, the No. 2 carried the tripod, and Nos 3, 4, and 5 carried ammunition, spare barrels, entrenching tools, and other items. For additional protection the No. 1 and No. 2 were armed with pistols, the remaining three carried rifles. This large team was often reduced to just two or three (as in this photograph), the gunner, the loader (also barrel carrier), and the spotter. The gunner of the weapon was normally a junior NCO.

(**Opposite, below**) Totenkopf troops in their winter reversibles can be seen unloading a 10.5cm howitzer off a flatbed railcar during the Battle of Kharkov. The 10.5cm light field howitzer was used extensively on the Eastern Front and provided the division with a versatile, comparatively mobile base of fire.

(**Above**) On the outskirts of Kharkov and grenadiers can be seen marching along a road towards a stationary Volkswagen Type 166 Schwimmwagen. It was near the city where Waffen-SS forces maintained a bridgehead between Volokomovka and Kupiansk on the River Oskol. The column of parked Schwimmwagen are from a Leibstandarte SS Adolf Hitler (LSSAH) reconnaissance battalion. This is a platoon of one of the motorized companies, which in 1942 had exchanged motorcycles for light, mobile cars.

(**Opposite, above**) Grenadiers in their winter reversibles grey side out hitch a lift aboard an armoured vehicle belonging to the II SS Panzer Corps as it negotiates its advance through the streets of Kharkov. The Battle of Kharkov was a series of battles launched by both the Waffen-SS and Wehrmacht that began on 19 February, to take advantage of the Red Army which was weakened and had overrun its supply lines following the massive series of offensives it had undertaken leading to its victory at Stalingrad.

(**Above**) Totenkopf troops moving through Kharkov. They all wear the reversible winter jacket and trouser grey-side out. The reversible clothing consisted of a heavy double-breasted overjacket for extra frontal warmth. It had double-buttoned overlaps to the flaps of the jacket to the front which when closed were wind-resistant. The bottom edge of the jacket had drawstrings attached, and the ends of the cuffs were adjustable as well. The trousers and jacket were thick. They were shorter than normal standard issue uniform trousers but could be either worn over the top of the leather marching boots or tucked inside. The ends of the trousers were gathered in by drawstrings and tied in around the boots.

(**Opposite, below**) German infantry can be seen standing on a road during a lull in the fighting. To the left is a captured Russian artillery piece.

A young gunner during operations somewhere on the Ost Front. He carries the MG tool box attached to his black leather infantryman's belt. A common method of carrying machine-gun ammunition is a ready-to-use belt draped around the neck with the bullets pointing outwards to prevent them digging into the body.

Gebirgsjäger troops appear to be using this temporary position to rest and use foliage from surrounding fir trees for protection against the arctic temperatures.

A Waffen-SS light machine gun troop during winter operations. The troop was ideally a three-man crew, but due to the high casualty rate sustained in Russia this was commonly reduced to two. In the distance part of a battery of StuG.IIIs can be identified on the move.

(**Above**) A whitewashed Pz.Kpfw.IV can be seen halted in the snow. This camouflage paint was designed to be thinned with water. It could easily be washed off by the crews in the spring, exposing the dark grey base colour. Not all the crews received the whitewash paint and had to adapt and find substitutes to camouflage their vehicles. Some used lime, some chalk, others used white cloth strips and sheets, and even hand-packed snow. Mud too was sometimes used. Vehicles with no camouflage at all were sitting targets.

(**Opposite, above**) A photograph taken from the cupola of a Sturmgeschütz III showing regular soldiers and men from the 7th SS 'Prinz Eugen' covering a hole on a road with wood to allow their column to continue its drive.

(**Opposite, below**) Panzerjäger troops with a whitewashed Pak35/36 anti-tank gun during a fire mission. The soldiers are all wearing the M1938 field cap, which perhaps suggests this photograph was taken not under battlefield conditions but in training.

A troop leader in his winter whites, whitewashed steel helmet and black woollen toque is armed with the MP40 machine pistol. He is wearing mittens. Soldiers often wore special mittens with a separate trigger finger, normally worn over woollen gloves.

Two crew of a whitewashed Pz.Kpfw.IV can be seen with their vehicle. By the mid-war period the German army had developed a new revolutionary item of clothing for the armoured crews called the parka. The parka was well-made, well-padded and kept crews warm. Initially it was first designed in field grey with a reversible winter white (as this photo depicts, worn both white side and grey side out by the crew). But by late 1943 a modification was made replacing the field-grey side with a camouflage pattern, either in green splinter or tan water. The coat was double-breasted with the interior set of buttons being fastened to provide additional protection.

(**Opposite, above**) A Waffen-SS gunner stands next to his camouflaged 7.5cm PaK40 in the snow. This gun was compact and when dug in and well concealed it presented a very small silhouette to the front. Like the PaK38, the PaK40 had a spaced-armour shield held together by large bolts.

(**Above**) A soldier armed with a Karbiner 98K bolt action rifle oversees the removal of captured Russian soldiers from a shelter.

(**Opposite, below**) During a pause in the fighting a well-positioned whitewashed PaK40 trains its powerful 7.5cm barrel across a snow-covered field. This gun was more than capable of disabling heavy Soviet tanks.

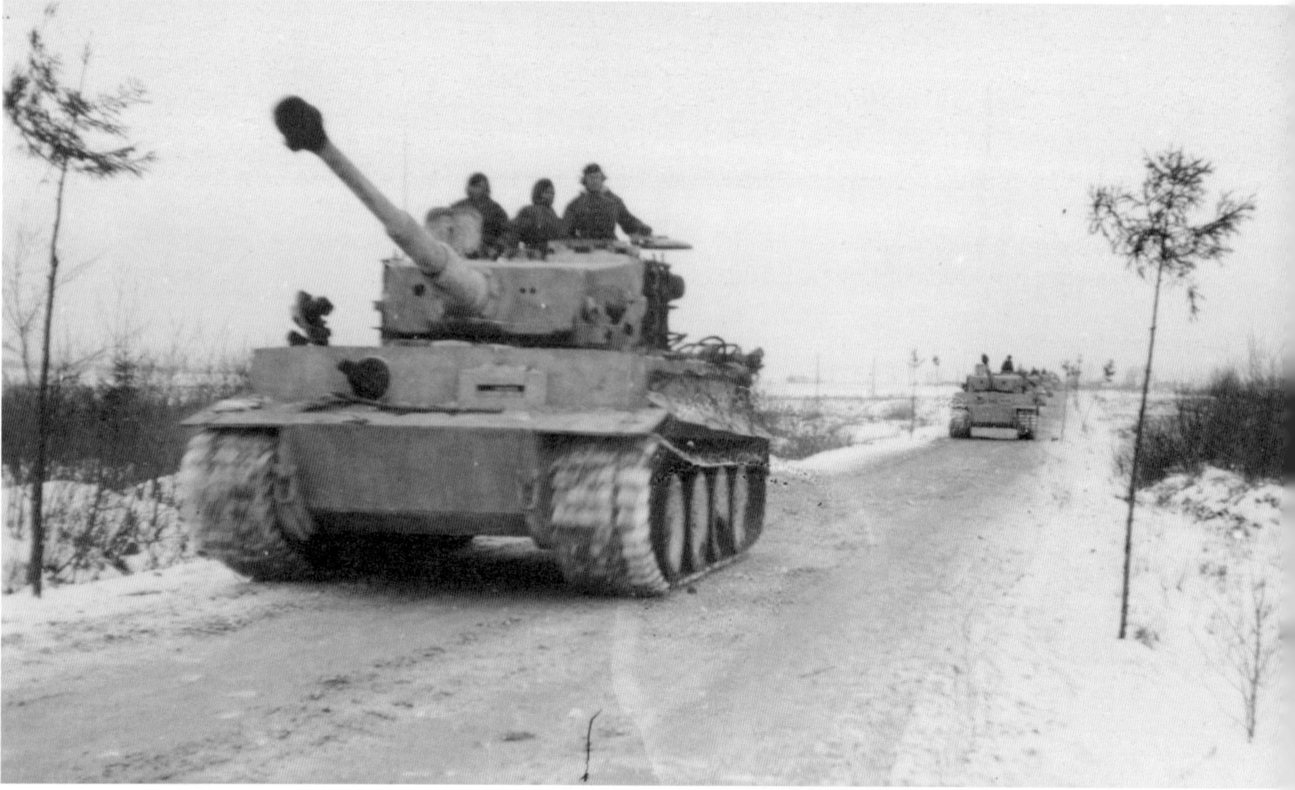

(**Opposite, above**) One of the wheels of this 10.5cm le.FH.18 light field howitzer appears to have fallen through some ice on a road and become stuck. The Waffen-SS crew are trying to pull it out using a length of timber.

(**Opposite, below**) A Tiger I rolls along a Russian road during the late winter of 1943. For the Tiger crews the hard frost made travelling much easier than rain or thaw. Even after the failed Kursk offensive, winter operations that year still saw heavy Tiger tank battalions demonstrating their awesome killing power on the battlefield.

(**Above**) A group of troops from von Manstein's Army Group Don pose for the camera before operations. All are wearing the reversible grey/white two-piece winter suits.

(**Above**) Here the gun crew of a whitewashed 7.5cm PaK40 move the weapon into position. The PaK40 was considered far from light, especially when the crew had to manhandle it in the snow or muddy conditions. This one has taken six men to move it into position.

(**Opposite, above**) Troops during operations in southern Russia can be seen with a 7.5cm Geb36. Firing an artillery piece in the snow could be frequently problematic. The recoil would regularly drive the weapon deep into the snow which could cause inaccurate firing. For this reason the 7.5cm Geb36 gun was modified for winter combat in the snow. In this photo the gun's wheels have been removed and replaced with sturdy gun trails.

(**Opposite, below**) Troops preparing a new position in what appears to be a former Russian trench. These small trenches were a standard Soviet trench design and generally provided cover only if a soldier stooped.

(**Above**) A well concealed PaK gun. The weapon has been covered with snow and the 7.5cm barrel camouflaged with white sheeting. The gunner is wearing an animal-skin greatcoat and a crude attempt has been made to partly camouflage his helmet with some white cloth.

(**Opposite, above**) A group of Pz.Kpfw.III crew members pose for the camera in front of their whitewashed vehicle. They wear a variety of winter clothing ranging from a greatcoat, to reversibles grey and white side out. Three of the men wear the black panzer field cap under a hood, the other two wear the Ushanka fur cap with ear flaps down.

(**Opposite, below**) During a winter operation this flak crew are using their 2cm Flak gun against a ground target. Note the gunner's Flakvisier 35 sight and the way in which it is lined in elevation to the gun tube.

Out in the snow is a whitewashed 8.8cm Flak 18 gun being readied by its crew for action. This was the most famous German anti-aircraft gun of the war. It was bolted on a cruciform platform from which it fired with outriggers extended. Here the crew have used the weapon for ground attack. The 8.8 proved very versatile and continued in use until the end of the war. Note the gun's limber positioned nearby.

Winter clad grenadiers advance across a snowy field supported by a whitewashed Pz.Kpfw.III.

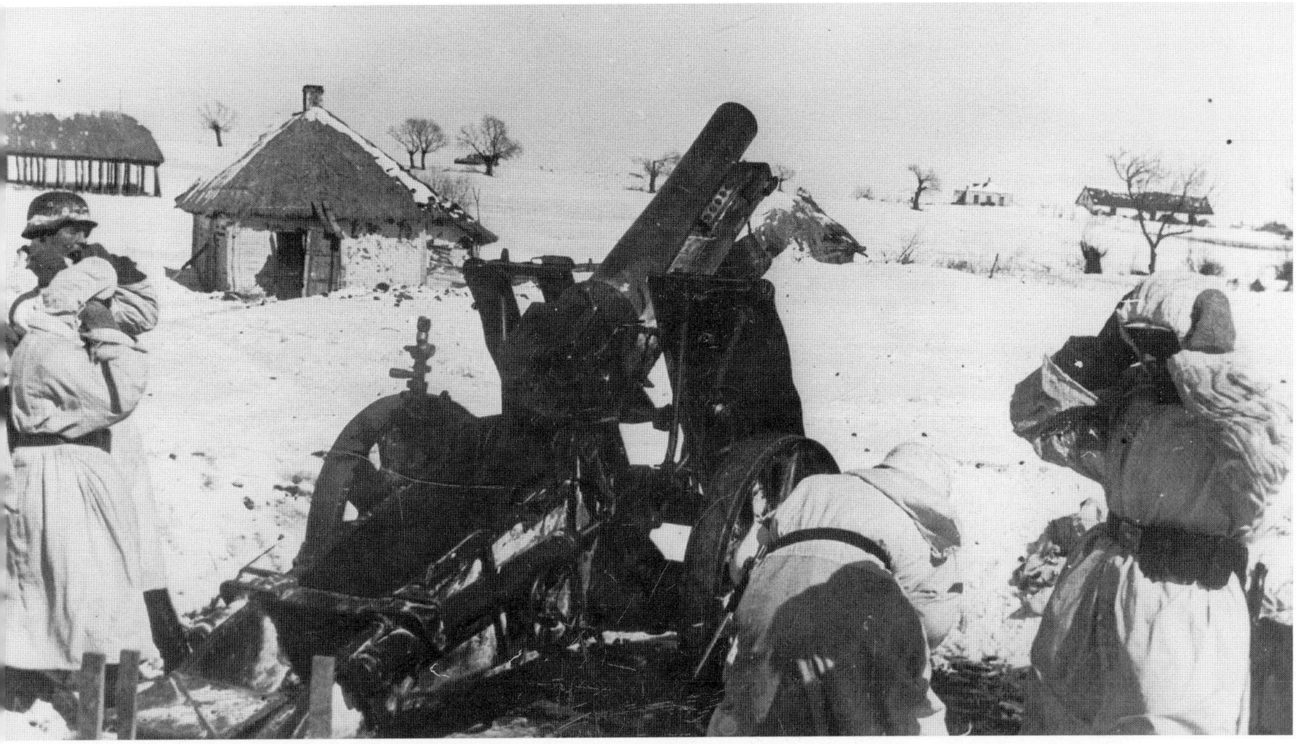

The crew of an uncamouflaged 15cm sIG33 protect their ears as the gun is fired during an attack against Russian positions. The crew are all wearing white snowsuits and blend well with the local terrain. Although the clothing was far superior to that issued in the first winter, frostbite and hypothermia still caused many casualties.

A converted Pz.Kpw.II Sd.Kfz.131 Marder II during winter operations on the central front. This vehicle was designed with a high profile and its open-topped armour had minimal protection for the crew. Inside the vehicle two crew members wear their winter reversibles grey side out; their commander is donned in the familiar standard Sturmartillerie uniform without any winter protection.

A troop leader converses with his men with the aid of a map during operations in late winter 1943.

At a forward observation post and a soldier during a reconnaissance mission can be seen with a light-weight radio complete with ear phones.

(**Opposite, above**) Waffen-SS soldiers in a remote winter position recover a parachute-dropped provisions bomb with up to 200lbs of supplies. Inside these 'bombs' were rations, ammunition and medical supplies. These containers were painted orange and had a white parachute canopy.

(**Opposite, below**) A flak crew, all wearing their winter whites, preparing their weapon for a fire mission against a ground target.

(**Above**) Defending a flatbed train, probably part of an artillery unit, an MG34 crew can be seen with their weapon in an anti-aircraft role. The troops wear green splinter pattern camouflage smocks. As with most of the later version winter camouflage smocks these uniforms proved extremely comfortable. They also gave the wearer plenty of freedom of movement as well as concealment.

Chapter Four

The Fourth Winter 1944/45

The military situation on the Eastern Front in January 1944 was extremely dire for the German army. It had entered the New Year with a dwindling number of soldiers to man the battle lines. The Red Army on the other hand was now stronger than it ever was before. Hitler refused to concede territory, and there was a persistent lack of strategic direction in the East. Meanwhile the soldiers were compelled to fight on.

In Army Group North, divisions had been trying in vain to hold their positions from the Volkhov River to the Gulf of Finland with a string of trenches and shell holes reminiscent of the First World War. On 15 January 1944 the defences were attacked in another offensive by three powerful Soviet fronts, the Leningrad, Volkhov and Second Baltic. The 18th Army, which bore the brunt of the attacks, were outnumbered by 3:1. Overwhelming fire power proved too much for the Germans and they were compelled to fall back. In four days the Russians had breached Army Group North's defences in three places. This opened a corridor allowing the Red Army to pour through towards the besieged city of Leningrad. On 26 January, Leningrad was liberated after 900 days of siege.

The entire German northern front subsequently began to crumble. As the weather began to slightly improve in February, morale was temporarily restored and units gained enough strength to hold back the Red Army. However, during March the Russians began exerting more pressure, especially against the 16th Army that was defending positions along the Baltic. As the spring thaw arrived, the melting snow turned the roads into quagmires, and Soviet tanks could be seen sinking up to their turrets in mud. The German front line appeared to be holding, with the weather playing a major part. It would not be until early summer that the Red Army would resume its push.

Meanwhile, for Army Group South the conditions were dismal. Supplies were inadequate and replacements in men were far below what was really needed. At the start of January, despite fighting through freezing winds and blizzards, a 110-mile breach between Army Group Centre and Army Group South had developed.

Neither group had sufficient forces to plug the gap and by the end of the month it had opened even wider when the Belorussian Front pushed the 2nd Army to the Dnieper River.

By this time German mobile reserves had been worn down to almost extinction and this led to a number of units being encircled. One of the largest pockets to develop was in the Kovel-Korsun area of the lower Dnieper where seven German divisions and the premier 5th SS Wiking Division were trapped. By using their remaining Panzers, they drove a wedge and created a corridor for the encircled men and held it open to allow them to escape. Some remnants of the shattered divisions broke out and struggled south-east under continuous Russian fire.

To the north of Korsun the situation was equally dire. The worn out 1st and 4th Panzer armies were all that were left to support troop operations in the south, and they were being slowly pressed against the Carpathian Mountains. In early March, as the snow and ice melted, advanced Soviet units reached the outskirts of Tarnopol and within days Red Army troops advanced through the city. Defending Tarnopol were German units that had been given instructions to defend all towns to the death. These suicidal assignments were nicknamed Himmelfahrts-Kommnandos (missions to Heaven).

In Tarnopol conditions were appalling. For days the Germans held out inside the ruins under sustained bombardments from Soviet artillery. As Russian infantry attacked through the streets and fought house to house, the defenders reported that the scenes were reminiscent of Stalingrad. For the next three weeks four thousand soldiers held out. When a rescue mission by the 9th SS Division tried to relieve the trapped force, only fifty-three men managed to break out and reach the German lines. The rest were captured or killed.

In spite of the casualties and losses of equipment inflicted upon Army Group South, its forces had defended its positions well during the winter of 1944. In fact, in some places it even held the line.

By the end of March the crisis in the south was temporarily relieved as the Russian winter offensive gradually died away. However, the Russians were preparing for a huge summer offensive against the German centre which was to carry them to the banks of the Vistula in Poland. The offensive, Operation Bagration, saw the destruction of Army Group Centre in July 1944 and caused a chain reaction of events that led to a succession of collapses on the Eastern Front.

By August, Red Army forces were fighting in Poland. Further north along the Baltic the bulk of the German forces had withdrawn from Estonia and were being threatened in Latvia and Lithuania. In early October Riga was captured, which infuriated Hitler, who ordered the evacuation of thousands of troops and 100,000 tons of materials to the Kurland bridgehead. In total some thirty divisions would be moved to the Kurland area where they were ordered to dig in and fight to the death to defend what remained of Latvian territory in German hands.

Fighting in Kurland raged. The Red Army had collected some sixty divisions for the purpose. The attack was to coincide with the massive offensive being prepared against the remnants of Army Group Centre that were now holding the banks of the Vistula in Poland.

Further south-west, in mid-October 1944 the Soviets launched a winter attack into East Prussia, the First East Prussian Offensive (also known as the Gumbinnen Operation). The Russians, comprising the 3rd Byelorussian and 1st Baltic Fronts, were met by strong resistance, and the offensive was brought to a standstill in the region of Ebenrode. In spite of the losses, Gumbinnen was taken on 22 October, but it was retaken by German forces two days later after they brought up reinforcements from the 5th Panzer Division and Heavy Panzer Detachment 505 equipped with new Tiger IIs.

Over the next few days the town was again taken by Russian units, and then recaptured yet again by the Germans. A stalemate of sorts then reigned and further action was postponed until reserves could be mustered. This would commence when the Russians launched their winter offensive several weeks later.

The Soviet offensive begun in the third week of January 1945. The principal objective was to crush the remaining German forces in Poland, East Prussia and the Baltic states. Along the Baltic an all-out Russian assault had begun in earnest across snow and ice, the intention being to crush the remaining understrength German units that had once formed Army Group North. It was these attacks that eventually reduced German-held territory in the north-east to a few small pockets of land surrounding Libau, Kurland, Pillau in East Prussia and Danzig at the mouth of the Vistula.

Here along the Baltic the German defenders attempted to stall the Russian push with the remaining weapons and men they had at their disposal. Every German soldier knew the significance of their task. Hitler made it clear that no-one was to evacuate but had stand and fight, thereby condemning to death 8,000 officers and more than 181,000 men.

In south-west Poland on the Oder the strategic town of Breslau had been turned into a fortress and was defended by various Volkssturm, Hitlerjugend, Waffen-SS and other formations from the 269th Infantry Division. During February 1945 they defended the town with every available weapon, but in the first week of March Russian infantry had entered city and were pulverising it street by street. The Russians lost 60,000 killed or wounded capturing the town, the Germans lost 29,000 defending it.

Elsewhere along the Eastern Front the February and March weather prevented the soldiers digging trenches more than a metre deep. Worse than that were the extreme shortages of ammunition, fuel and vehicles. The ration was two shells per gun per day.

Tens of thousands of under-nourished civilians, mostly women and slave labourers, were marched out to dig anti-tank ditches between the Vistula and Oder rivers. German forces were barely holding the wavering positions that ran 175 miles from the Baltic coast to the junction of the Oder with the Neisse. In the north, Stettin, capital of Pomerania, and in the south Küstrin, were vital holding points against the main Russian objective: Berlin.

By the end of March the German forces that were now known as Army Group Vistula were manned by mostly inexperienced training units. Boy soldiers had sweets instead of tobacco in their rations. All were ordered to stand and fight to the death. Retreat would mean almost certain execution. The only hope was that the Soviet attackers would give them a chance to surrender instead of burning them alive with flamethrowers or blowing them to pieces with hand grenades.

When spring came and the icy roads thawed the Germans were already defeated. The Red Army broke across the Oder River and Seelow Heights and headed for Berlin. The end of the war was only weeks away.

Winter-clad grenadiers armed with the deadly Panzerfaust can be seen before an operation. During the last year of the war the Panzerfaust was used extensively to combat Russian armour. It was a handheld rocket-propelled grenade, effective at a range of about 90 metres.

A close-up of a whitewashed Pz.Kpfw.IV crew. The vehicle clearly has an application of Zimmerit anti-magnetic mine paste applied to the chassis and turret sides. By late 1944, Zimmerit was no longer being applied to new vehicles coming off the assembly lines.

An excellent view of a Sd.Kfz.251/9 mounting the short powerful 7.5cm KwK 37 L/24 gun. This halftrack wears the remains of a winter camouflage and mounts its radio antenna on the left side of the superstructure next to where the radio was repositioned when the gun was mounted. Spread across a snow-covered field, behind the vehicle, are two old 10.5cm field howitzers and a prime mover still retaining its summer camouflage scheme.

An infantry support vehicle has halted on a road and some of the troops have disembarked. Note the display of an infantryman's combat equipment, which generally consisted of the shelter quarter, canteen, bread bag, gas mask canister and entrenching tool. They also wear the rifleman's ammunition pouches for the general-issue Kar 98k rifle.

Out in the snow panzergrenadiers stand next to a Sturmgeschütz.III or StuG.III Ausf.G during operations in early 1944. An MG42 machine gun can be seen leaning against the vehicle. This vehicle is equipped with the longer barrelled 7.5cm StuK 40 L/48 cannon, which both necessitated modification of the frontal superstructure and increased the vehicle's weight to 21.3 tons.

Troops during a reconnaissance mission are seen wearing their winter whites. The soldiers can clearly be seen wearing the coloured friend-or-foe recognition stripes on their sleeves. Note how their winter whites have become soiled with dirt and grime.

A rare opportunity to see a whitewashed Sd.Kfz.251/22 advancing in the snow in northern Russia. This halftrack was armed with 7.5cm PaK40 L/46 auf Mittlerer Schützenpanzerwagen. Although the gun was too big for the carriage, and overloaded, it was still an effective weapon despite being outdated by 1944.

Along a snowy road a whitewashed prime mover can be seen towing the deadly 8.8cm flak gun towards the front. Of all the flak guns introduced into service one of the best-known and reliable weapons was the '8.8cm Flugabwehrkanone 18, 36 und 37' (8.8cm Flak 18, 36 and 37). All three versions were extensively used during the war by the Luftwaffe, Heer, and later the Waffen-SS. These three services also used another new 8.8cm Flak gun. It was known as the 8.8cm Flugabwehrkanone 41 or 8.8cm Flak 41 (Eisenerz). It was built specifically for a dual role and thus possessed a genuine anti-tank capability. Its longer 71-calibre barrel gave it an increased muzzle velocity and better penetration. In service it proved robust, reliable, and it continued in production until the end of the war.

Wearing their winter suits, panzergrenadiers can be seen hitching a lift aboard a StuG III. When a tank company went into action with infantry, there were normally two platoons on the line, one platoon at the rear, and a fourth in reserve. The interval between tanks was usually 300–360 feet.

Panzergrenadiers on the march in the snow moving along a road with a column of whitewashed Pz.Kpfw.IVs. In the last year of the war, the deciding factors in ground warfare were the Panzer, self-propelled artillery, and motorised infantry. The panzergrenadiers had become so important to the successful continuation of the war that seven of the thirty Waffen-SS Panzer divisions and six Panzergrenadier divisions became elite Waffen-SS formations. These seven divisions became Hitler's emergency 'fire brigade', with the occasional assistance from a number of less elite SS-Panzergrenadier Divisions.

Winter-clad motorcyclists with sidecar combination have halted at roadside. Advancing along the road is a Tiger I. It appears that the crew have used chalk or painted stripe marks over the armour and barrel in an attempt to conceal the conspicuous summer camouflage parts of the vehicle.

In a trench and Waffen-SS troops belonging to the Totenkopf Division are being subjected to Soviet aerial and ground bombardment. The Russians continued to pound German positions who were soaked, freezing and exhausted. The Totenkopf fought on, but were overwhelmed by enemy superiority both in numbers of soldiers and weapons. To prevent being totally destroyed, a general retreat by Totenkopf and the SS-Wiking Division ensued, much to the anger of Hitler. Following the loss of Hungary, the bulk of the Waffen-SS withdrew into Austria to defend Vienna. Totenkopf helped in the defensive battle around the Austrian capital.

A Panther appears to be towing a halftrack along a muddy road during operations in the winter of 1944.

A Kübelwagen halted on a muddy road near Vinnitsa. These vehicles were a staff, utility and reconnaissance car.

Two photographs taken in Vinnitsa on the Eastern Front showing Tigers belonging to the I SS Panzer Korps negotiating a muddy road.

(**Opposite**) Two photos showing soldiers riding in an Sd.Kfz.2, the Kleines Kettenkraftrad HK 101, or what the Germans called Kettenkrad. Initially this vehicle was a motorcycle tractor for airborne units or Fallschirmjäger, but later served in Heer and Panzerwaffe units. The vehicle was primarily tasked with laying communication cable from a special mounted wire spool. However, the vehicle could be used for a variety of other tasks such as pulling heavy loads and carrying fast-moving troops. Later in the war the Kettenkrads appeared in reconnaissance patrols and independent scout detachments and were used especially where roads were almost impassable due to mud.

(**Above**) A long column of whitewashed Pz.Kpfw.IVs advancing along a snow-covered road. Some of the crew on board are dressed in the army issue camouflage splinter reversible jacket and trousers, which were not widely issued to Panzer crews.

(**Opposite, above**) SS Panzergrenadiers donned in their SS winter parkas hitch a lift aboard a Pz.Kpfw.III during a fighting withdrawal. The tank has clearly seen some enemy contact as it is missing some of its side-skirt.

(**Opposite, below**) An interesting photograph showing a Panther Ausf.G from the 1/SS Panzer-Regiment 1 of the 1.SS Panzer-Division 'LSSAH' photographed during its operations in Hungary in February or March 1945.

(**Above**) Panzergrenadiers hitching a lift aboard a Panther on a road somewhere on the Eastern Front.

A well-camouflaged 8.8cm flak gun. Its barrel is in a horizontal position, ready at a moment's notice to be used against possible ground targets. In some sectors of the front, units barely had enough tanks to oppose Russian armour and called upon flak battalions to halt the Red Army's attacks.

Panzergrenadiers in their winter whites being transported by Sd.Kz.251 halftracks across the snow. By this late period of the war many infantry divisions had been redesignated as Panzergrenadier divisions. Although having an armoured designation, the Panzergrenadier division was still technically an infantry formation. However, unlike a normal infantry division there was a higher than usual attachment of armoured vehicles. A typical Panzergrenadier division had at least one battalion of infantry that were transported to the forward edge of the battlefield by Sd.kfz.251 halftracks, and various armoured support provided by its own StuG Battalion.

The workhorse of the German divisional artillery was the 10.5cm le.FH18(M) seen here during a fire mission. Three members of the artillery crew wear the green splinter pattern camouflage smocks.

Panzergrenadiers advance across a stream during a fighting withdrawal operation in the winter of 1945. The wear and tear of the winter season's fighting is demonstrated on their tattered and wet insulated suits. Sometimes the troops had no opportunity to wash their suits or themselves for weeks or even months.

Two soldiers wearing green splinter pattern camouflage smocks with fur caps. One appears to be drinking a bottle of vodka and his comrade reaches out for a taste.

The final defence. Troops being shown how to use the Panzerfaust during defensive actions in March 1945. More than half of the tanks knocked out in combat during the Soviet drive into Germany were destroyed by Panzerfausts or Panzerschrecks. The high loss became such a concern that the Red Army began installing spaced armour on their tanks. Each tank company was also assigned a platoon of infantry to protect them from infantry anti-tank weapons.

Appendix One

Taschenbuch für den Winterkrieg (Paperback for the Winter War)

Below is a translation of the contents of the winter warfare handbook:

Section I. **WINTER, MUD, AND THAW**

1. INFLUENCE OF WINTER
2. DURATION AND NATURE OF SNOW
3. SEASONS OF MUD AND THAW
4. PREPARATION FOR WINTER WARFARE
5. WINTER COMBAT METHODS
6. MORALE
   a. General
   b. Recreational Aids
      (1) *Reading material*
      (2) *Lectures*
      (3) *Radio*
      (4) *Movies*
      (5) *Employment of 'Strength through Joy' groups*
      (6) *Competitions*
      (7) *Improvement of quarters*
      (8) *Organisation of spare time*
      (9) *Service centres*
      (10) *Front convalescent camps*

Section II. **MARCHES AND ORIENTATION**

7. MARCHES
   a. Reconnaissance
   b. Preparation for Marches
   c. March Discipline
   d. Halts and Rest Periods

Section XII. EVACUATION OF WOUNDED

48. GENERAL
49. MEANS OF EVACUATING WOUNDED
    a. General
    b. Hand Sleds and Improvised Means
50. EQUIPMENT OF VEHICLES FOR WOUNDED

Section XIII. CARE AND USE OF WEAPONS AND EQUIPMENT

51. GENERAL
52. LUBRICANTS
53. RECOIL LIQUIDS
54. CARE OF WEAPONS
    a. Rifles and Carbines
    b. Semiautomatic Rifles
    c. Pistols
    d. Submachine Guns
    e. Machine-Gun Equipment
    f. Machine Gun (MG34)
    g. Antitank Rifles
    h. Tank Guns
    i. Antiaircraft Guns (2cm Flak 30 and 38)
    j. Artillery
    k. Chemical Mortars and Heavy Projectors
        (1) *105mm chemical mortars 35 and 40*
        (2) *Heavy projectors 40 (wooden model) and 41 (metal model)*
55. FIRING OF INFANTRY WEAPONS
    a. General
    b. Rifle
    c. Light Machine Gun
    d. Heavy Machine Gun
    c. 50mm Light Mortar 36 (5cm l.Gr.W. 36)
    f. 81mm Heavy Mortar 34 (8cm s.Gr.W. 34)
    g. Infantry Howitzer
    h. Antitank Weapons
56. STORAGE AND HANDLING OF MUNITIONS IN WINTER
    a. Storage
    b. Ammunition in Combat Positions
    c. Handling of Shell Cases
    d. Ammunition of Chemical Troops
    e. Special Experiences

64. SKIS, ACCESSORIES, AND SNOWSHOES
   a. Skis
   b. Ski Shoes
   c. Army Flat-Terrain Ski Binding
   d. Overboot
   e. Ski Kit
   f. Snowshoes
65. HAND SLEDS
   a. General
   b. Akjas
   c. Construction of Light Akja
   d. Construction of Hand Sled
66. HORSE-DRAWN SLEDS
   a. General
   b. Army Sleds
   c. Loading Army Sleds
   d. Toboggan Type of Sled
   e. Runners and Sliding Troughs
      (1) *Runners*
      (2) *Sliding troughs*
   f. Drags
   g. Harnessing
67. PACK HARNESS

Appendix Two

The Eastern Medal

The Eastern Medal (officially the 'Medaille Winterschlacht im Osten 1941/42') was in acknowledgment of what the Germans referred to as 'a probation of struggle against the Bolshevik enemy and the Russian winter between 15 November 1941 to 15 April 1942'.

The medal could also be awarded posthumously to any soldier who died in the line of duty on the Eastern Front. It was nicknamed by the troops the 'Frozen Meat Medal' (Gefrierfleischorden).

Over 3 million were issued. It was later to include both male and female combatant and non-combatant personnel. Foreign members of Wehrmacht units were issued with the medal until it was decommissioned in September 1944.

Notes

Notes

Notes